Book 1 - chap 1-3
Book 3 - chap 3-6
Book 4 - all 1-5, 7-8
Book 5 - all

ELDERS' TRAINING

THE MINISTRY OF THE NEW TESTAMENT

BOOK 1

WITNESS LEE

First Edition, 6,000 copies, December 1985.

Library of Congress Catalog
Card Number: 85-81865

ISBN 0-87083-112-7 (hardcover)
ISBN 0-87083-113-5 (softcover)

Published by

Living Stream Ministry
1853 W. Ball Road, P. O. Box 2121
Anaheim, CA 92804 U.S.A.

Printed in the United States of America

CONTENTS

FOREWORD

During February of 1984 over three hundred and fifty brothers from six continents gathered in Anaheim, California with Brother Witness Lee for a two week international elders' training. The messages that were released at that time are the contents of this four volume set. Book one presents the essential aspects of the ministry of the New Testament; book two sets forth the vision of the Lord's recovery; book three covers the way to carry out the vision; and book four emphasizes other crucial matters concerning the practice of the Lord's recovery.

Those of us that were in these meetings were deeply convicted of our need to be further enlightened by the Lord concerning God's economy and concerning the intrinsic essence of the New Testament ministry which is for the carrying out of this divine economy. As the Lord's recovery is continually spreading throughout the world, these messages are more than crucial and urgently needed. We believe that they will render a great help in preserving all the saints in the central lane of God's economy, without any deviation, for the fulfillment of His eternal plan. Our hope and expectation is that these messages will become a governing and controlling vision for all in the Lord's recovery. May we prayerfully consider all the points presented in these books and accept them without any preferences.

November, 1985   Benson Phillips
Irving, Texas

CHAPTER ONE

THE ONENESS OF GOD'S MINISTRY AND THE PERIL TO IT

OUR PRAYER FOR THIS TRAINING

Lord, we need You, and we need You to have mercy upon all of us. Lord, we thank You for Your sovereign environment. You have brought us all together; Lord, we thank You for this gathering, and we believe it is of You. We believe, Lord, that You have a purpose for this gathering. We do treasure this time. Lord, be with us.

We thank You, Lord, for Your cleansing blood. This is what we trust in every day. Lord, we are still so natural, so full of the old creation. Too much we have been living in ourselves or doing things in the flesh. Even our view, Lord, our purpose, our motive, and our intention are altogether impure. How much, Lord, we need Your cleansing, the cleansing of Your redeeming blood. We thank You, Lord, for the redeeming blood. Lord Jesus, even in our service to You, our activities for You, the work we have done is impure. We are so impure, Lord; we need Your cleansing. Cleanse us thoroughly. Lord, we have regret for the past, and we repent to You of all the things. Lord, we still take You as our sin offering and our trespass offering.

Lord, we come together to look unto You that we may receive mercy and find grace to meet our timely need. Lord, we need You; we need You to grant us a further visitation. Lord, open the heavens and clear the sky. Even, Lord, open Yourself to us. We are looking to You and to Your speaking, to Your unveiling, and to Your deep, deep work within us.

O Lord Jesus, we can do nothing, and we have nothing. Lord, everything is entirely up to You. Lord, give us the willingness, and make us ready. Lord, purify our intentions, and purify our heart. Give us a sober mind; even, Lord, give us a seeking and open spirit. Lord, do cover us. We trust in Your prevailing blood. Lord, defeat the enemy for Yourself, for Your recovery, and for these two weeks of this training. Lord, defeat him in me every day. Lord, keep us in Your presence. Amen, Lord.

OUR BURDEN FOR THIS TRAINING

In our burden to see the Lord's present move among us in His recovery, we need to consider twelve main items, beginning with the ministry of the New Testament. Second, we need to see what the up-to-date vision in the Lord's recovery is. Third, we need to see the way to carry out this vision, which is a very crucial matter.

Fourth, we will fellowship about the use of reference books. The Lord's testimony has been on this earth for over nineteen centuries. Many saints have been very much used by the Lord, and many of them have written something. The way we will use those books is a major consideration that has very much to do with our present work and surely affects this work either profitably or not profitably. We need a thorough consideration of how to use the reference books.

In addition, we will fellowship about the regions of the ministry, and about the relationships between the regions of the ministry and the local churches. These are items number five and six. Seventh, we will consider the Chinese-speaking work and the Chinese-speaking meetings. This has been raised up by the Lord's move, especially in recent months. Therefore, we need to consider how we should cooperate with the Lord's move in this matter. Eighth, we need to fellowship about the matter of publications for the Lord's ministry.

Furthermore, we need to spend more time to fellowship

about the elders' position and function. We need to reconsider, to review, and to thoroughly get into the matter of the elders' position and function. This is the ninth item. Tenth, we need to fellowship thoroughly about the damages of control. Then we will fellowship about the liberty of the saints.

As the last item, we need to fellowship again concerning our attitude toward the denominations and the free groups. In other words, we need to reconsider what our attitude should be toward our fellow Christians, the fellow believers who are not meeting with us.

GOD'S MINISTRY

When we come to the ministry of the New Testament economy, we need to see why the Apostle Paul emphasized the matter of the New Testament ministry so strongly in chapter three of 2 Corinthians. The word ministry is defined by the Apostle Paul very much in that chapter, which we have covered quite thoroughly in the Life-study of that book. Paul stressed the New Testament ministry in that chapter because he was strongly vindicating his ministry, which he called the ministry of the new covenant, compared with and in contrast to the Old Testament ministry, which he called the ministry of the old covenant. In 2 Corinthians 3 we can see that in God's eyes there are only two ministries in the entire Bible. One is called the ministry of the old covenant (vv. 7, 9, 14), and the other, the ministry of the new covenant (v. 6). The word covenant is actually the same as the word testament. It is more clear and more convenient for us to use the word testament because the two sections of our Bible use these two terms, the Old Testament and the New Testament. What we call the New Testament and the Old Testament, Paul calls the new covenant and the old covenant.

In the Bible, God only revealed to us two ministries, one of the Old Testament or the old covenant, and one of the New Testament or the new covenant. Actually, these two ministries are one, just as the Old Testament and the New Testament are one Bible with two parts or two sections. The Bible means the Book, and it denotes God's holy writings, the Holy Scriptures. The Scriptures also mean the writings, so all of these terms refer to the same book. God does not have two Bibles; He has only one Bible with two sections, the Old Testament and the New Testament. In the same way, God's ministry is actually one with two sections, the old section and the new section. The Old Testament was a preparation for the New Testament which was to come.

After much study of the holy Word and after many years of laboring in the Lord's Word, we can see today that God's ministry is to use His chosen vessels to carry out His economy, that is, to fulfill His eternal purpose by dispensing Himself into His chosen people that they may express Him. For the accomplishment of His economy, God needs men as His chosen vessels.

THE PRINCIPLE OF INCARNATION

According to the divine principle, although God is able to do everything to carry out His economy and He will do everything for this purpose, He will not carry out His economy by Himself apart from man. The principle for God to accomplish His economy must be the same as the principle of incarnation. The principle of incarnation is very great. God is surely able to save the fallen people. Because He is God and He is sovereign, He is able to do everything. Nevertheless, He has a divine principle—He must do everything concerning His economy in the principle of incarnation. The principle of incarnation requires that God enter into man to make man one with Him. Therefore, man is a vessel for the mingling of God and man.

Even in the Old Testament, we see the principle of incarnation. Nevertheless, it was hard for God to make a type of incarnation. Only in creation did God do everything by Himself, apart from man, apart from the principle of incarnation. In God's work to produce the old creation, the first creation, man had no share because he had not yet been created. When man was created, everything else had already been created. Therefore, man had nothing to do with God's creating work.

However, to carry out His economy, God depends upon His second creation much more than on His first creation. His first creation resulted in physical materials but it was not God's intention merely to create the old things and stop there. His intention was to go from the first creation to the second creation. It is by the second creation that God accomplishes His economy. In God's second creation nothing has ever been done nor will be done without man. God does not accomplish His economy apart from man, and man cannot accomplish it himself. It can only be accomplished by God mingled with man.

The first case, the first instance, the first accomplishment, of God's economy was by Jesus Christ. We need to see who this Jesus Christ was for the first accomplishment of God's economy. He was neither only God nor only man. He was both God and man, a God-man. Although God is altogether mighty and altogether able, He cannot accomplish redemption without man. Apart from man, He cannot do anything to accomplish His economy in the second step, the step of redemption. In the first step, in the old creation, He did everything by Himself, but in the second step He can do nothing apart from man. In the second creation it is necessary for Him to be one with man and to make man one with Him, not in adding Himself to man, but in mingling Himself with man.

The very conception of the Lord Jesus of the Holy Spirit, the conception of the incarnation, is itself a mingling. A conception of any kind cannot take place without mingling. Therefore, we should not listen to the traditional, so-called theological teaching against mingling. Actually, the strong ground for the teaching of the divine mingling is the divine conception.

Incarnation is a conception that equals a mingling of God with man, a mingling of divinity with humanity. This mingling produces a God-man, a holy One who is both God and man. This holy One is the complete God and the perfect man, and He was the first One used by God to accomplish His economy. He was the beginning. Following Him is His reproduction, His increase, His continuation. This reproduction, this increase, this continuation, is corporate. This is His Body, a composition of all the members who all are the reproduction, increase, and continuation of that unique One who is both God and man. In principle, we are the same. Therefore, it is altogether scriptural and necessary to say that we are God-men, according to the principle of incarnation, a principle kept by God to fulfill His economy.

THE ONE MINISTRY

In the Old Testament there was a ministry for the preparation of the New Testament economy. Actually, the Old Testament ministry and the New Testament ministry are one. The Old Testament ministry was a preparation, a shadow, a prefigure, and the New Testament ministry is the fulfillment. What took place in the Old Testament was a shadow of what would take place in the New Testament ministry. Therefore, the New Testament ministry is the very fulfillment of the Old Testament ministry.

I am burdened to stress this point of the oneness of the ministry because of all the divisions and confusions that have taken place in the past centuries among the Christians. The most damaging thing among the Christians is the divisions and the confusions. Moreover, all the divisions and confusions came out of one source, and that source is the different ministries.

In the Old Testament there are thirty-nine books with the accounts of different services, but these different services do not constitute different ministries. There is the service of the priesthood, of the kingship, and of all the prophets. It is true that the word service equals the word ministry in Greek, but in our present language we need to use different words to denote different aspects. In order to make this matter clear, we need to use these two different words, the ministry and the service, or the services. Everyone would have to agree that there was only one ministry in the Old Testament. The priests, the kings, and the prophets all bore the same one ministry in different aspects of service. Some, including Aaron and Melchisedek, served in the priesthood. Some, including David and Solomon, were in the service of the kingship. Nevertheless, their different services were all for that unique ministry. In the same principle, Isaiah and Jonah served as prophets, yet they accomplished God's unique ministry. God did not have two ministries in the Old Testament, but He had one ministry definitely called the ministry of the old covenant, according to the word of the Apostle Paul in 2 Corinthians 3. That ministry was a figure of the real one that was to come.

The reality of the one ministry, the ministry that fulfilled the figure of the old covenant ministry, did not actually begin from the Lord Jesus, but from John the Baptist. First there was John the Baptist, then the Lord Jesus, then the twelve disciples, and then so many others from Acts to Revelation. In all of these ministers the New Testament bears or unveils only one unique ministry, a ministry to carry out Christ to bring forth the church. Eventually the unique ministry of God is to carry out the ministry of Christ that the church might be brought into being. Christ and the church are the central subject of the entire Bible. This is the center, the focus, and also the circumference of God's economy. Christ and the church must be everything in God's economy. To carry out this economy, God has only one ministry, a unique ministry. Of course, the service of John the Baptist was different from that of the Lord Jesus. The service of the Lord Jesus laid a foundation for the service of the apostles. The apostles accomplished a service which occupies the great part and the main part of the New Testament ministry to accomplish God's economy.

DIVISIONS COMING OUT OF DIFFERENT MINISTRIES

Why is it that there were divisions even from the time while the apostles, including Paul and John, were still here on this earth? Divisions began to take place from the last part of the first century and have continued to take place until the present century. There have been divisions after divisions, which have caused all kinds of confusion. What is the reason for all these divisions? They all came about simply because of different so-called ministries.

As those in the Lord's recovery, we must ask ourselves what our realization is of the Lord's ministry to carry out His economy. What is our view concerning the damages that have been brought in through the so-called different ministries? Today every denomination has its own ministry. To be a preacher in a certain denomination, it is necessary for you to be limited to a certain kind of ministry, limited in your teaching, in your preaching, in your doctrine, and even in your behavior. In every denomination, you need to be limited to the ministry of that particular denomination.

We need to be very clear that the foundation of all the denominations and the factor that produces each denomination are their different ministries. If all the Christians today would be willing for the Lord to take away their different ministries, they would all be one. The basic factor of all the divisions, their very root, is different ministries. Ministries that are different may be very sound, even very scriptural, but they are something Paul said was creeping in at the time of Galatians 2 (v. 4, lit.). This thing crept in as early as the time of Paul. Paul, Peter, and James were all there, and a ministry of another kind was trying to come in. In 1 Timothy 1 Paul charged Timothy to remain in Ephesus to take care of one thing: to charge certain ones not to teach differently, which means not to teach according to another ministry (vv. 3-4). At that time the different teaching was the teaching of the law. In Galatians 2 what was trying to creep in was the law.

At a later time, the heretical teaching of Gnosticism came in. Gnosticism was heresy, but you cannot say that to teach something of the Old Testament was heretical. At this point we need to consider that whole situation carefully. Paul was carrying out God's New Testament ministry and his ministry followed Peter's ministry, which was an immediate continuation of the ministry of the Lord Jesus Himself. In the four Gospels Jesus Christ carried out God's ministry, and in the first part of Acts, Peter continued that ministry. Then in the second part of Acts, Paul's ministry was a continuation of Peter's to carry out God's New Testament ministry. Nevertheless, when the Judaizing believers were strong in teaching the law, Peter became weak. Peter was afraid of those who came down from James (Gal. 2:11-12). This also indicates that James was a strong figure, a strong character, in tolerating the teaching of the law in the New Testament age.

Can you imagine Paul facing that problem? In Antioch Paul was facing the number one apostle, Peter, and he was facing representatives of the most influential apostle, James. It was not easy for Paul to face that situation. Two strong influences were there, the influence of Peter and the influence of James. Peter could have said to Paul, "Who are you, Saul of Tarsus? When I was speaking there in Jerusalem, you were still a young man opposing. Who do you think you are?"

In addition, Paul was facing the representatives of James, a godly man who prayed so much, day after day, that there are reports that his two knees were calloused. James was famous for his godly perfection and was very influential. He became even more influential than the great first apostle, Peter. Peter was afraid of his influence. In Antioch Peter was eating with the Gentiles peacefully. However, when some representatives came from James,

Peter became a hypocrite and pretended that he had not eaten with the Gentiles. This indicates how strong James' influence was.

Paul, as a younger apostle who had come later than Peter, was facing such a situation. Undoubtedly, it was hard for him. Nevertheless, for the sake of the truth, Paul did not tolerate that situation. He did not allow such a thing. He cut off the different ministries. He closed the door for the different ministries to creep in, and God honored what Paul did in that situation.

According to the New Testament and according to church history, from that time onward Peter did not play an important role in God's New Testament economy, not as important as the role he played in the first twelve chapters of Acts. This is an important point. After not too long a time, in A.D. 70, God destroyed Jerusalem (Matt. 24:1-2), which was the base of Peter's work and the base of James' influence. He tore down the whole thing, leaving no stone upon another, destroying it. Not only was that a judgment on the rebellious Israel, but it was also the destruction of the base of Peter's work and of James' influence. After the destruction that took place in A.D. 70, however, Paul's ministry and his influence remained. God did not allow different ministries and other influences.

We need to see this principle throughout the entire Christian era. All the troubles, divisions, and confusions came from the one source of the tolerance of different ministries. Many Christian teachers have known the peril of different ministries; nevertheless, they have tolerated them. There has been a tolerance of different ministries. In the Lord's recovery, for the long run, we should not believe that this kind of creeping in of the different ministries would never take place. Rather, we must be on the alert. Such a peril is ahead of us. If we are not watchful, if we are careless, in one way or another the enemy would creepingly use some means, some ways, to bring in different ministries. Such a thing would end the Lord's recovery.

One hundred fifty years ago the testimony of the Brethren was unique, and it was very strong. However, it was damaged by one thing: different teachings. They neglected Paul's word to Timothy to charge certain ones in Ephesus not to teach differently (1 Tim. 1:3). The Brethren were very good in dividing the Word. Actually, this was their main teaching, according to 2 Timothy 2:15. Nevertheless, they neglected one crucial verse concerning God's economy in Paul's Epistles to Timothy. In 1 Timothy 1:4 the word economy, or dispensation (*oikonomia*), is strongly used, and Paul charged Timothy to take care of God's economy.

All of us today need to be on the alert. We need to realize that Satan could use any one of us to bring in some other kind of teaching that may be scriptural. At Paul's time it could not be considered heretical to teach the law according to the Old Testament. The law had been given by God and unveiled by God. If I had been there teaching Gnosticism, then I would have been a heretic. On the other hand, if I had been there teaching the law of Moses, no one could have said that my teaching was heretical. In fact, the law of Moses was scriptural. Nevertheless, such teaching would have been different from the teaching concerning God's economy as it was presented by Paul. We need to be very careful because Satan is subtle. All of us need to be alert not only to watch over others but to watch over ourselves.

When I speak such words of warning to all the dear saints, I speak them even the more to myself. Many times I have seen something new that had to be considered very carefully in the light of the Lord's up-to-date ministry. I need to consider very carefully whether or not each item is something of God's ministry today. Each point must be measured according to God's basic economy. How to measure every point, how to make a decision about every item, all depends upon God's basic economy, which is to carry out the ministry of Christ for the producing of the church.

If we keep this one basic principle and one basic factor concerning God's economy, we will be well protected. Nevertheless, each one of us needs to be on the alert not to watch over others but to take care of ourselves that we would not be used by the enemy to bring in different thoughts or different teachings that may seem to be scriptural.

CHAPTER TWO

LESSONS CONCERNING THE ONENESS OF THE MINISTRY

At this point we need to spend some time to be brought into the New Testament ministry so that we may see this ministry from the beginning to the end of the New Testament. It is crucial for us to see what the New Testament ministry is. We have already pointed out that the New Testament ministry began with John the Baptist. However, we should not consider his ministry a separate, individualistic ministry. The ministry of John the Baptist was a part of the New Testament ministry. It was a service of the New Testament ministry, even the first service of that ministry. We need to look into this ministry in a particular way to pick up a crucial point.

When we come to the Lord's appraisal of His forerunner's ministry in Matthew 11, we can see that even that first service, that first part of the New Testament ministry, was a unique ministry. John's ministry of repentance, the way of repentance, was a very striking ministry that drew the line between the Old Testament and the New Testament. That ministry was a landmark in God's economy. Nevertheless, John's ministry should not be considered as a separate, independent, individualistic ministry. If you had such a consideration, you would become what the Gospels call the disciples of John.

A RIVALRY TO THE LORD'S MINISTRY

In Matthew 9 the disciples of John came to question the Lord Jesus, and they included the Pharisees along with themselves in their question (v. 14). According to Luke 5, it was the Pharisees who did the questioning (v. 33), and according to Mark 2, it seems that the diciples of John and the Pharisees questioned the Lord together (v. 18). Before that time, the Pharisees were one sect, and there was another sect, a heretical sect, called the Sadducees. However, at the time of Matthew 9 the disciples of John became yet another sect. From this we can see that probably not more than two or three years after John began to preach, his service caused trouble and became a rivalry to the Lord's ministry.

God did not intend that John's service would become a separate ministry. In God's intention, John's service was simply the beginning of the New Testament ministry, a recommending service that initiated the Lord's ministry. John told us clearly what his ministry was (John 1:23; 3:28-30), but his disciples understood in a wrong way. They thought that their teacher, John the Baptist, was great and that his teaching was unique. They followed him, and they followed his teaching. Perhaps unconsciously and unintentionally, they became a rivalry to the Lord's ministry. Eventually that preaching became something replacing the Lord's ministry.

Quite often we fail to recognize the Lord's sovereignty in the things that happened to John the Baptist. First Herod put John into prison, and then, due to Herod's indulgence in lust, he had John beheaded. However, we need to realize that for John to be put into prison was sovereign of the Lord, and even for John to be beheaded was sovereign of the Lord. I certainly do not mean to say that God was happy to see John imprisoned, much less to see him beheaded. Nevertheless, we must believe that God is sovereign, and we need to consider soberly why God allowed John to be imprisoned and later beheaded.

The imprisonment and execution of John came about because there was a care for another ministry. John's ministry and his diciples caused some trouble. First, God

stopped John's preaching through Herod. Then even from
the prison John sent his disciples to the Lord Jesus with
certain questions. Right after that, John suffered martyr-
dom. God was sovereign to terminate what was there with
John at that time. Of course, that termination was not a good
or positive termination.

The case of John the Baptist shows us that there is a peril
that we may receive a genuine ministry, a genuine service
from God, and yet we would not be willing to see that service
terminated. This is a crucial point. God may use you, and He
may use me. He may use us for a certain service with a view to
His purpose, but after we have been used by Him, probably
none of us would be willing to see the termination of that
service.

The same principle can be applied in the case of Moses.
The account of the shining of Moses' face in Exodus 34 does
not tell us why Moses covered his face with a veil (vv. 30-35).
However, according to Paul's interpretation in 2 Corinthians
3:13, Moses was afraid that the people would see the termination of his ministry. Moses did not want the people to see the
shining of his ministry come to an end. Even in his case there
was a consideration about the termination of his ministry. We
all are happy to be used by the Lord in a certain service, but
none of us would be willing to see that service come to an end.

It was this kind of trouble that forced God, the sovereign
One, to allow John to be imprisoned and even to have his life
terminated. We need to consider this whole matter carefully.
Without God's sovereignty to allow things to be carried out in
this way, surely the teaching of John would have been taken
over by his disciples and would have created a big problem.
Here we need to learn the lesson. God would not allow any
ministry, any service, to remain in a rivalry with His New
Testament ministry. What happened in the case of John the
Baptist sovereignly cleared up the whole situation. For the
rest of the time of the Lord's ministry, there was no rivalry,
but there was opposition. Opposition is comparatively easy
to deal with, but it is very hard to deal with rivalry.

God tolerated the opposition from the Pharisees for a longer time, at least up until A.D. 70, when Jerusalem was destroyed. The Lord even prophesied that not one stone of the temple in Jerusalem would be left upon another because of their opposition, their rejection of Him, and He indicated that the temple of God had become their house because they had made it a den of robbers (Matt. 24:1-2; 23:38). The Lord tolerated the opposition for a number of years, but He did not tolerate the rivalry. Immediately John was put into prison, and his life was terminated. We need to learn the lesson from this case. This matter is something of the Lord's sovereignty.

THE CONTINUATION OF THE
NEW TESTAMENT MINISTRY WITH PETER

After John the Baptist, the Lord Jesus continued God's New Testament ministry, and He thoroughly accomplished that part of the ministry. Then the day of Pentecost came. On that day Peter was strong, and he was pure in every way. In chapters two through five of Acts we can see a young man, probably still in his thirties, clean and very pure in every way, in intent, in desire, in motive, in the heart, in the spirit, and in the understanding. He had no consideration about anything other than the Lord's ministry, even no consideration about his life. With him at that time there was no problem in any point.

Peter and the Old Testament Way

However, in Acts 10 Peter's attitude caused a problem for God; it troubled Him. In Matthew 16 the Lord told Peter that He would give him the keys of the kingdom. There are at least two keys because the word keys is plural. On the day of Pentecost Peter used one of the two keys to open the gate for the Jewish people to enter into God's New Testament kingdom. However, when God was going on to use him with the second key to open the door for the Gentiles this contradicted Peter's background and tradition. On the day of Pentecost all that was necessary was for the Holy Spirit to descend upon Peter, but for the house of Cornelius God used two visions, one vision to Peter and another vision to Cornelius. This indicates that God was troubled because He was forced to take the Old Testament way of visions and dreams. The New Testament way is to follow the anointing within, to follow the indwelling Spirit. Peter had the Spirit dwelling within him inwardly, but he could not understand the indwelling because of his background and his tradition. Peter had the outward outpouring of the Spirit and also the inward indwelling of the Spirit, but he could not understand the indwelling. This is a crucial point.

To carry out God's ministry there is the need of a clean person. How clean Peter was on the day of Pentecost and in chapters two through five of Acts! Nothing was there as a veil covering him, and he was absolutely pure as crystal. But after a short time, even when he was praying in Acts 10, there was a veil covering him. That veil was tradition and his Jewish background, covering him and keeping him from the New Testament way. Nevertheless, God overcame him, subdued him, and even convinced him to go to the house of Cornelius to use the second key to open the door for the Gentiles to come in.

The Termination of Peter's Ministry in Acts

We need to read and reread Acts with much consideration. After Peter used the second key, Acts 12 tells us that he was put into prison, and then released from prison. Nevertheless, after Acts 12 there is nothing in Acts 13 concerning Peter. Chapters thirteen through twenty-eight are for Paul, and in Acts there are no more chapters for Peter. Peter's ministry was finished in the New Testament ministry of God in Acts. Peter was good, and I believe he wrote both his Epistles after this time. (The date of 1 Peter is uncertain, whether before or after the time of Acts 13.) It was very good that Peter wrote those two Epistles. Especially in the second one, he was very genuine and bold, because he recommended one who had rebuked him to his face (2 Pet. 3:15-16).

After Acts 12, we do not see Peter until chapter fifteen. However, in Acts 15 Peter was no longer the first among the apostles nor even the first among the elders in Jerusalem. At that time in Jerusalem the atmosphere, the tendency, and the influence were not in favor of Peter, but were altogether in favor of James, who somewhat might be considered a semi-New Testament apostle, a great part New Testament and some part Old Testament.

Elements of Mixture

Something colored gray can blend in either with something colored white or with something colored black. James can be compared to something colored gray, something that can fit in with either side. Peter should have been compared to something pure white, but he did not dare to be what he was. Under that atmosphere, influence, and tendency, what Peter was would not have been welcome. However, James was welcome because he could fit in with two sides at the same time.

From what we have seen in the Life-studies of James and Mark, we can realize that even the situation in Acts 15 was not entirely pure. We need to see the decision that was made in Acts 15 in the light of what happened in Acts 21. Although "it seemed good to the Holy Spirit" (v. 28), that decision was made mainly under James's influence, and it was not purely according to God's New Testament economy. What happened in chapter twenty-one came out of the decision that was made in chapter fifteen. In other words, we could say that the weakness that was there in chapter fifteen was exposed in chapter twenty-one. In Acts 21 James was very bold to declare that there were tens of thousands of Jewish believers in Jerusalem zealous for the law (v. 20). James was even so bold that he advised Paul to take the same way.

THE TURN OF PAUL'S MINISTRY

We may say that Paul became weak in Acts 21 and

followed the advice of James. Some may argue that Paul was not weak, but that he was very strong to keep his word that to the Jews he became a Jew (1 Cor. 9:20). They may excuse Paul, but the Lord did not allow him such an excuse. We know the Lord did not excuse Paul because on the last day of the vow that Paul had agreed to participate in, He brought the whole thing to an end. Paul had paid the charges for the poor votaries, and with just one more day they could have completed the vow. However, the Lord did not allow such a thing. As a result, all of Jerusalem was brought into an uproar, and Paul was arrested and put into prison.

This matter is very serious. Even Paul's ministry was turned at this point because there was some involvement there. We should not get ourselves involved in things of this kind. It is altogether a serious matter to weaken God's economy or to make it gray. As for Paul, he was pure, and God was, therefore, able to use him in another way, to write the Epistles. It was very good for Paul to write the Epistles, such as Ephesians, Philippians, and the others written while he was imprisoned. Nevertheless, the writing of these Epistles was all of Paul's ministry after Acts 21. These are serious matters.

THE CASE OF BARNABAS

We need to go back to consider something concerning the case of Barnabas. He was faithful, and he was the one who brought Paul in (Acts 9:27). He was also a companion apostle to Paul. However, he had an opinion. To us, that was not a serious matter. Surely Barnabas was not a Judaizer, but because of his opinion, he took his way to carry out the so-called ministry. That was the termination of the record concerning Barnabas in the book of Acts. Not only in the Bible, even in history it is hard to trace any record concerning Barnabas after this point. What a sober word this is for us today!

THE PROBLEM OF APOLLOS'S MINISTRY

Then at the end of Acts 18, Apollos came in. He came neither from the source of Peter nor from the source of Paul, but from some other source. We cannot trace from what source Apollos came, but he appeared in chapter eighteen, teaching the Scriptures and knowing only the baptism of John (Acts 18:24-28). It was necessary for Apollos to be merged in with Paul's ministry, the more the better. Although he may have been very much one with Paul, his case became a problem.

In Corinth Apollos became a problem, and Peter became a problem. I could not find out whether or not Peter himself had ever gone to Corinth. However, his ministry became a problem there, not because of Peter, but simply because there was such a thing as Peter's ministry. There was a following of Peter's ministry since there were those who said, "I am of Peter" (1 Cor. 1:12). Apollos was also there, and there were those who said, "I am of Apollos." I do not believe that Apollos had any intention to cause trouble, but the trouble came, not because of Apollos, but because of his ministry and its following. Paul was a man in the Spirit, and he did not condemn Peter, nor did he condemn Apollos. Rather, in speaking things negatively, he mentioned his own name first (1 Cor. 1:12). We need to consider these matters carefully to see the peril that is before us today. In Corinth, Peter's ministry and its following and Apollos's ministry and its following created a problem that almost caused a division.

Suppose I were Apollos. In such a case, do you think the Lord would use me more and more? If I had a ministry that was used as Apollos's, do you think that my usefulness to the Lord would be increasing all the time? Paul's ministry was never used in that way. His ministry was the major item in God's New Testament ministry. Such was not the case with the ministry of Apollos.

In any case, at Corinth there were problems due to these three kinds of service, that of Peter, of Apollos, and of

Paul. I do not believe that Apollos conducted himself in a way to be one with Paul to the uttermost in God's New Testament economy (see 1 Cor. 16:12). He was not divisive, and he did not separate himself from God's New Testament ministry. Nevertheless, we could not see in the Scriptures that Apollos was one hundred percent one with Paul in God's New Testament economy.

A PERSONAL TESTIMONY

Allow me to testify something from my experience in working with Brother Watchman Nee. I worked with Brother Nee for over eighteen years. There are some among us who were there at that time and did see the situation. Since the beginning of Brother Nee's work, a number of prominent Christians who later became famous preachers were there with Brother Nee for a time. The first meeting of the Lord's table in the Lord's recovery took place with Brother Nee and another brother and his wife. These were the three who initiated the Lord's table meetings in the recovery. Eventually that brother became a problem to Brother Nee because he was not one with him in God's move at that time in China. From that time on, one prominent brother after another came in to the recovery there in China. Nearly all of them became problems to Brother Nee. If I had taken the same attitude as the others, surely I would have become a problem to him also. However, all realized that I was one thousand percent one with Brother Nee in his ministry because my standing, my attitude, and my spirit were altogether one with him. No opening was left for anyone to say that I was a problem to Brother Nee. There was no ground for such a charge.

If someone is able to ask you whether or not you are one with me, that question is a hint that you are not one hundred percent one with me. If water can leak through a roof when it rains, that surely means there is a crack somewhere in the roof. If there is no crack, no water could leak in. If you are thoroughly one hundred percent one with me, we are like a roof that has no crack for the rain to come in. When it rains, the water both testifies and tests whether or not there is a crack in the roof. If there is a leak, this is a proof that a crack is there.

THE PROBLEM IN CORINTH AND THE PERIL TODAY

We need to read the facts in the Bible, not merely the letters in black and white. There was a reason for the problem in Corinth where some said, "I am of Cephas," "I am of Apollos," and "I am of Paul." If Peter had behaved, acted, and worked in an atmosphere, in color, and in flavor absolutely one with Paul, no one at Corinth would have said that he was of Peter and not of Paul. If Apollos had been working, preaching, moving, and living in a way that was with the flavor, the color, and the atmosphere that absolutely matched that of Paul, no one would have said that he was of Apollos and not of Paul. There were three entities there. One was of Peter, one was of Apollos, and one was of Paul.

Whether you call them three ministries, three leaders, three headships, or three different kinds of teaching, the fact that there were three created a leak for the rain to come in, and the rain did come in. Some were saying, "I am of Peter. I don't care for Paul." Others said, "I am of Apollos. I don't care for Peter or for Paul." Still others said, "I am for Paul." Therefore, in Corinth there was fighting among the saints that came from the different flavors, different colors, and different atmospheres of the so-called ministers. If Peter, Apollos, and Paul were working, moving, and walking in one atmosphere, in one color, and in one flavor, I do not believe anything could ever happen in Corinth that would cause the people to say that they were of this one or of that one. Such a thing could happen there simply because the atmosphere, the flavor, the color, and the spirit among the three were not one.

Then how about our situation today? We need to consider our present situation soberly according to this light from the Scriptures. Again I say that I would have much more liberty to speak concerning these matters if Brother Nee were working among us. If this were the case, he would be the target instead of me. Because I am the target now, it is hard for me to speak concerning certain matters, lest whatever I say be considered a self-vindication.

Nevertheless, all of us need to realize that we are in the Lord's recovery. The first characteristic of the Lord's recovery is oneness. Once we lose the oneness, we are through. If we lose the oneness, we are no longer the Lord's recovery. Therefore, we need to see that there is a peril of different teachings and different opinions damaging the oneness. I thank the Lord for His mercy that since the beginning of His recovery in this country I have never been so cautious in any other matter as I have in this one matter. In all these twenty-three years it has been my practice to exercise myself never to debate with any of the brothers concerning doctrines or concerning opinions. Six years ago some very serious problems arose among us. During that time, you probably did not hear me say anything concerning these problems because I did not want to give any impression that I was open to debate concerning the opinions and doctrines of others. However, this did not mean that I agreed with those opinions and doctrines. Now I realize that the more we are going on, the more we are in a trend with a peril that opinions and different teachings may come in. Opinions may be good, and teachings may be scriptural, yet they may be different. Sooner or later, these matters will create a hidden division. The blessing that always comes down from God to His recovery is based upon the oneness (Psa. 133). If we lose the oneness, we will lose the blessing.

I believe that we can learn from Apollos's case that there is the possibility of having different flavors, different atmospheres, and different colors, although we may move together, minister together, work together, and all be together in the Lord's recovery. Apollos was not dissenting with Paul, but his ministry bore a different color and flavor than Paul's ministry.

I am not saying that something has already happened among us to create a problem. No storm has come, but a weather report has. In the climate of the Lord's recovery today, there are some signs that some storms may come if we do not exercise our carefulness. For this reason, I am burdened to present the real situation to you in order that you may realize that there is a peril ahead of us. Even though we are not in any storm yet, I do feel the need to send out the weather report to let you know that there is the possibility of storms coming in this climate if we are careless. I hope we would not have a repetition of the storms that came six years ago. I believe all of us have a good intention. I do not believe there is anyone among us with a wrong intention. Nevertheless, the things we do could be wrong even though our intention is not wrong. All of us need to be careful.

OUR ONE CONCERN
—GOD'S ECONOMY, NOT DOCTRINE

When I was with Brother Nee, I never behaved, acted, worked, preached, taught, or spoke in any way that could be taken by the enemy to create trouble. Please be clear that what I am saying does not mean that I was one hundred percent in oneness in every doctrine with Brother Nee. For example, my interpretation of the two witnesses in Revelation 11 even today is different from that of Brother Nee. I believe Brother Nee was influenced by Pember, Govett, and Panton, all of whom interpreted the two witnesses as Enoch and Elijah, based on the statement in Hebrews 9:27 that a person can only die once. Enoch and Elijah were the only two persons who did not die; therefore, it was interpreted to mean that they were preserved by God in order that they could be the two witnesses in Revelation 11 who would be killed there.

Although I never told anyone, from the first day I heard

this interpretation, I felt strongly that it was not accurate. In the first place, God has a testimony in the Old Testament that is constituted of the law and the prophets, the law represented by Moses and the prophets represented by Elijah. Therefore, in the New Testament, even according to the Jewish way, the Rabbinical way, the Old Testament was called the law and the prophets even by the Lord Jesus Himself. In Revelation 11 the two witnesses stand before the Lord, and they bear a testimony. In this universe we see these witnesses standing before the Lord on the Mount of Transfiguration—Moses and Elijah.

In addition, if we say that man could only die once, based on Hebrews 9:27, we need to account for the case of Lazarus. He died once, and he was resurrected. Then he died a second time. There is also the case of the son of the widow in Nain (Luke 7:11-15). He died and was being carried in a coffin when the Lord Jesus came and raised him up. He was resurrected, but he surely died again. In the Scriptures a number of persons died twice (1 Kings 17:17, 22; 2 Kings 4:32-35; 13:21; Matt. 9:24-25; 11:5; Acts 9:40; 20:10).

Surely you can realize that I was not following Brother Nee blindly. I have given you a little hint that I did not necessarily agree with Brother Nee in every point of doctrine. You would have to agree that my so-called dissenting point is logical and scriptural. The major points concerning the two witnesses were covered in message twenty-seven of the Life-study of Revelation, pages 317 through 325. Those points are very basic. Fact is fact, and the truth is the truth. However, I do not care for such things as whether the two witnesses are Elijah and Moses, or Elijah and Enoch. My one concern is for God's economy, for Christ and the church. Never have I found a person who surpassed Brother Watchman Nee in the matters of Christ and the church. For this reason, I placed myself one hundred percent at his feet to follow him. Actually, in following him it was the Lord's economy that I was following.

NOT DAMAGING THE MINISTRY

My point, dear saints, is that we are not here for doctrines, but we are here for God's economy. For me to speak concerning these doctrinal points today does not cause any damage at all to Brother Nee's ministry. However, if I had said something concerning these matters while he was living and I was working with him there, there would immediately have been division. For this reason, I did not preach anything that Brother Nee did not preach, and I did not teach anything that he had not touched.

I do not feel at all ashamed to say that whatever I taught and whatever I preached was Brother Nee's. It is glorious that there was such a man on this earth who was worthwhile for me to follow. Nevertheless, I fully realized that Brother Watchman Nee was a man. If any knew his shortcomings and his weaknesses, I must be one of them. I treasure what the Lord is doing in using him to fulfill His purpose to the uttermost. I have no interest in doing a light work according to the religious practices of today. I consecrated myself and my future for God's unique purpose on this earth. I saw this purpose in Brother Nee, I was for this, and I sacrificed everything for this. Therefore, I would not say a word, and I would not do anything at all to damage this purpose. I saw that he was one used by God for God's purpose.

We should not forget the account of the rebellion of Miriam and Aaron (Num. 12:1-15). Surely they saw Moses' weakness. There is no question that Moses married an Ethiopian woman. However, when Miriam rebelled, she became leprous. She did not receive a reward; she had leprosy. This did not mean that Moses was not wrong. The point is that all of us need to be very careful. It is my practice to exercise care with all of you, and I do not believe that I have done anything to damage your being used in the hand of the Lord. Even the more, I have exercised care to help you be perfected that you may be used in the hand of the Lord. It is not at all a small thing to say a word or to do something to affect the Lord's recovery in a negative way.

I have always realized that it is a very serious matter even to affect the Lord's recovery a little bit, no need to say to damage it. I have been with one brother for over twenty-two years. I am very frank with him, and we are very close. Nevertheless, I have the assurance that even this brother cannot say that I have been so free to say anything to him about any brother that was not so positive. This does not mean that I have been blind, that I have been dumb, or that I have no feeling, just like a piece of marble. Rather, if you have feeling, I do believe at least I have it too. Yet I have never talked, and I have never said anything, because I am not here for that. Over fifty-five years ago I gave myself to the Lord, I came to this country, and I am still laboring day and night through all the hardships, absolutely for the Lord's recovery. I long to see all of you completed and perfected in the hand of the Lord that He may use you and that His recovery could be carried on in a prosperous way.

We are not here to repeat the history of Christianity or to do a religious work. We are here for the Lord's recovery. I am not speaking something to threaten any one of you. The Lord knows. I am burdened to speak the fact, the truth, and to open up the real situation to you with the real peril. We are here, dear brothers, and we need to learn of the Lord concerning His economy, even as Paul said, with fear and trembling (Phil. 2:12). From the four cases we have considered, you could see the hints concerning all the things that caused trouble in the Lord's move. Not one of the four persons we have considered—John the Baptist, Barnabas, Peter, Apollos—is a negative person, nor even someone who is superficial. They were very solid, right, good, moral, spiritual persons with weight. All of them were solid and weighty, yet in certain crucial points they were not careful; they did not carry on their ministry with adequate consideration of the real situation in the Lord's move. If Apollos had given thorough consideration to the whole situation, surely he would have realized that he must be the same as Paul, one with Paul in the same atmosphere, color, and flavor. That situation caused Paul to be embarrassed to the uttermost and, in a sense, to make a fool of himself in order to vindicate himself (1 Cor. 1:13; 9:1). It was not the opposers, the criticizers, who created the trouble and embarrassed Paul, but such dear ones as Apollos and Peter.

How much we all need to treasure this opportunity to see these crucial matters. We all need to have a clear sky with a crystal-clear view that we may know what it is we are in and that we may have a clear view of the real situation.

Chapter Three

THE NEW TESTAMENT MINISTRY IN THE GOSPELS

Through all the Life-studies of the New Testament we have completed during the past ten years, the Lord has laid a basic foundation that will enable us to see something further at this time concerning the ministry of the New Testament. There is need of such a solid foundational work to see the ministry of the New Testament in the four Gospels, the Acts, the Epistles of Paul, the Epistles of Peter, the Epistles of John, and finally, the book of Revelation.

When we finish the Life-study of the entire New Testament, probably within one more year, I am burdened to have one full ten-day training with thirty messages to review all of the Life-studies of the New Testament. However, I consider that this is a golden opportunity to open up within these few chapters something of what is on my heart along this line. To get into the depths of these matters in a solid way, to get into the intrinsic essence of them, it is necessary to have this basic foundational work and also necessary to have a pure situation, a pure oracle for the Lord to speak. I believe we do have such a situation among us, and I therefore have no hindrance or reservation within me to keep me from pouring out something of what has been on my heart for a long time. It would take at least thirty messages to cover what is on my heart; nevertheless, within these few chapters we can touch some crucial points.

THE TWO MINISTERS IN THE GOSPELS

In the four Gospels, there are actually only two unique

ministers—John the Baptist and Jesus the Savior. The ministry of John was the initiation of the ministry of the Lord Jesus, and the ministry of the Lord Jesus was the main ministry in the four Gospels. Needless to say, we should neither despise nor even neglect John's ministry since it was a very solid initiation of the New Testament ministry. We need to consider these matters carefully in the light of the depth of the truth, not merely according to the letters in black and white.

THE MINISTRY OF JOHN

The ministry of John was a termination of the old creation, the old culture, the old religion, the old ordinances, and the old practices. We all need a deep realization that the intrinsic element, even the intrinsic essence, of John's ministry was altogether a termination of all things which existed prior to and until his time. When John opened his mouth to begin his ministry, it was God's intention to use that ministry to terminate everything that was in existence up to that time except Himself. The only One that could never be terminated and that never would need to be terminated was the Triune God Himself. When John stood up to minister, his ministry terminated whatever God had created, whatever had come into being.

The best way to terminate anything is to bury it, not merely to get rid of it. Such a termination through burial was the intrinsic essence of the initiation of the New Testament ministry. The main reason why we cannot take the way of the majority of today's Christians is that their way is not to terminate the things of the old creation, but rather to cultivate and even nurture and foster the things of the old creation.

John's ministry was a termination that led to a new beginning. God had no intention merely to terminate things. Our God is a God full of purpose; only one with no purpose would have terminated things for the sake of termination. God terminated the things with the definite purpose that the termination would lead to a new beginning.

THE INITIATION OF JESUS INTO HIS MINISTRY

That new beginning was there with the second minister in the New Testament, the Lord Jesus Himself. Jesus was initiated and ushered into His ministry by John's baptism. It initiated Jesus into His post to accomplish His ministry. While John was ministering to terminate everything, Jesus came into John's ministry, not to take over that ministry but to enter into it. The way Jesus entered into John's ministry was by accepting John's baptism; even He accepted the termination at that time.

We need to consider carefully the reason Jesus accepted such a termination. Jesus was the God-man. The divine conception of Jesus was one of the Holy Spirit, with the divine essence mingled with the human essence to produce this unique Person—a Person who is the complete God and the perfect Man. In the past four thousand years of human history, there had never been such a wonderful One, One who was conceived of the Holy Spirit with the divine essence mingled with the human essence to produce a God-man, One who was completely God and perfectly man. He was unique. He was a God-man. Nevertheless, we need to have a deep realization within us that in His constitution there was the essence of the old creation. In its essence His humanity belonged to the old creation. He was a man, a genuine human being, with a human will, with human emotions, and with a human mind. He was not some kind of phantom as the Docetists falsely taught (see note 3[1] in 1 John 4).

Jesus was a real man, and that man was called, in the Bible, flesh. "In the beginning was the Word,... and the Word was God.... And the Word became flesh" (John 1:1, 14). We need to take special note that John 1:14 does not say that this Word became a man, but rather says that this Word became flesh. Not only did flesh belong to the old creation, but it belonged to the fallen creation. Such a statement may cause you to ask whether the Word which was God became something fallen. We need to exercise much carefulness in answering such a question. Paul gives the answer to this question in Romans 8:3: "God sending His own Son in the likeness of the flesh of sin and concerning sin, condemned sin in the flesh." He uses three things to compose one explanation: the likeness, the flesh, and sin. Of course, flesh here is the central item, the basic item. Attached to it is sin, and related to it is likeness. Jesus became flesh, and flesh had become fallen by that time. However, He took only the likeness of the flesh of sin, the likeness without sin. Jesus took the form, the likeness, yet it was the form of something that belonged to sin. This crucial point is neglected by many. The flesh is of sin, and the Son of God did indeed become flesh (John 1:14; Heb. 2:14; 1 Tim. 3:16). However, He was only in the likeness of the flesh of sin, and had no participation in the sin of the flesh (2 Cor. 5:21; Heb. 4:15). This was typified by the brass serpent lifted up by Moses for the sinful Israelites (Num. 21:9; John 3:14). The brass serpent was in the form, the likeness, of the actual serpent, without its poison. The Lord Jesus was typified by a serpent in form, but only in form. There was no serpentine nature in that brass serpent.

It was such a Jesus who came into God's terminating ministry which was being carried out by John. He came into that ministry, and He accepted the termination. He was buried in that death water. It was not until that juncture that the Holy Spirit descended upon Him. Before the descending of the Spirit upon Him, He had already been conceived of the Holy Spirit and born of the Holy Spirit. He possessed the mingling of the divine essence with the human essence by the Holy Spirit. He was conceived in this way, He was born in this way, and He was born to be such a being. However, at this point, when He accepted the termination ordained by God, the Holy Spirit came upon Him to anoint Him. Right away He became One who was a mingling of divinity with the terminated humanity and anointed with the Holy Spirit. It is quite meaningful that incarnation gave the Lord Jesus humanity and brought Him into humanity, but John's ministry terminated that humanity. The purpose of this termination was to lead to a new beginning in resurrection. After His baptism the Lord Jesus was a resurrected person. According to the Old Testament type in Exodus, the holy ointment should not be poured upon any flesh (30:32). Immediately after His baptism the Holy Spirit as the holy ointment descended upon Him, that is, it was poured upon Him because His flesh was terminated, and He became a resurrected man. In other words, His humanity had been terminated and resurrected.

THE UNIQUELY QUALIFIED MINISTER
OF THE NEW TESTAMENT

After the Holy Spirit descended upon the Lord Jesus, He was the qualified minister of the New Testament ministry. John was qualified, but in comparison with the Lord Jesus, John was not so thoroughly qualified. John was qualified only to a certain degree. John was not such a person as the Lord Jesus was. John was not a person conceived and born of the Holy Spirit with the divine essence mingled with the human essence. Only Jesus uniquely was such a Person. To the uttermost, what John had was a pouring out of the Spirit upon him.

Luke tells us that John was to be filled with the Holy Spirit, even from His mother's womb (1:15). According to the black and white letters, when we read that John was filled with the Holy Spirit, we presume that to be filled means to be filled within. Actually this is not the case. When the one hundred twenty were filled with the Spirit on the day of Pentecost, that filling did not mean that the Holy Spirit entered into them, but it meant that the Holy Spirit descended upon them (Acts 2:4). Not only John the Baptist but also his mother Elizabeth and then his father

Zachariah experienced such a filling of the Holy Spirit. John was the first one to be filled with the Holy Spirit in the New Testament. In that family the son took the lead, the mother followed, and the father concluded this filling of the Spirit. The entire family was anointed by the Holy Spirit. Nevertheless, John did not have the intrinsic thing within him as Jesus did. Jesus had something intrinsic that was conceived of the Holy Spirit with the divine essence mingled with the human essence. That intrinsic element is the basic difference between John's conception and birth and that of Jesus.

AN INDESCRIBABLE LIFE AND MINISTRY

All of us need to grasp this basic point that after His baptism and the Holy Spirit descending upon Him, Jesus became such a being with divinity and with humanity, but with a humanity that had been terminated and resurrected. After He was anointed, He began to minister. It is crucial for us to see what it was that He ministered. The four Gospels present His ministry to the readers, but many readers do not realize adequately what the four Gospels present.

Most readers only realize that the four Gospels are a biography, telling the stories of one life. Some good students of the Bible may present some spiritual teachings, doctrines, out of this biography. All of us need to see what the purpose of God is in presenting these four Gospels to us. These four were selected by the Holy Spirit out of many gospels that were written (Luke 1:1). It is very meaningful that these four were selected and all the others were not qualified. In these four Gospels that were selected out of so many we have a clear picture of the ministry of this unique One. Such a ministry is hard to describe.

In recent days we had a conference on Christ, the Spirit, life, and the church. In those messages I pointed out that there are no human words available in any language to describe the wonderful One whose life is recorded in these four Gospels. When Christ came out to minister, He acted, He lived, He worked, He moved, and He ministered in such a way that no vocabulary in any language can describe. Language depends upon culture. If there is a certain kind of culture, surely there will be language to match it and to convey it. However, in all of human history and all of human culture, there had never been such a One as this unique One, and there had never been such a life as the life of this One. Therefore, there is no vocabulary available for us to describe Him. Human eyes had never seen such a One or such a life. Therefore, there are no human words adequate to describe this One or His life. You cannot find one adjective in any language which is adequate to describe the One presented in the four Gospels.

In the Gospel of Mark

Even you cannot find a single adjective adequate to describe the life portrayed in the sixteen chapters of the Gospel of Mark, which has been somewhat disregarded by many Christian readers. Not many Christian readers respect Mark as much as they do John, Matthew, or Luke. In the Life-study of Mark we have seen a life that human words cannot describe. We could say that this life is a holy life, a divine life, an ethical life, a godly life, a righteous life, a life that is right both with God and with man, but none of these words is adequate. No philosopher ever invented a term that can describe Christ's character. We could say that He was loving, humble, kind, meek, mild, but again none of these words is adequate. A life is portrayed in the Gospel of Mark that stood out uniquely. You can only see it, but you cannot describe it because of the shortage of human language. No adjective can adequately describe this Person, the life He lived, the way He moved, the way He worked, the way He acted, and the way He ministered. No words are adequate, but a picture is presented which we have seen in the Life-study of Mark.

This One was willing to be under God as a slave. He

served God, and He took care of God's house, of God's chosen people. All of them got lost, and He took care of the lost household of His Master, the very God. Again, we are short of vocabulary to describe the way He took care of them.

By the Lord's mercy, we have picked up all the elements of His ministry in our human words, in human expressions that we can understand: to preach the gospel, to teach the truth, to heal the sick, to cast out demons, to cleanse the lepers. We do have words such as these in our human language, and this is all that we can understand. Yet there is something further that we cannot utter. In the notes on each of these items we saw that to preach is to announce the glad tidings to the miserable people, to teach is to shine upon the people in darkness, and to cast out demons is to destroy Satan's kingdom and release God's people. However, after we have said all that we could say, even with much consideration, we realize that there is still something more that we cannot utter concerning this wonderful One and the life He lived. Not only is it true that with Him you cannot find any fault, any shortcoming, or any wrongdoing; even you cannot find words adequate to describe Him on the positive side. Surely He was humble, patient, and enduring, but there is also something that we cannot put into words. When we have exhausted our human vocabulary, there is still something more.

Furthermore, it is clear that the Lord Jesus would never let His followers go, especially Peter, James, and John. We have covered this point in the Life-study of Mark. Whatever He did, He did with them. Wherever He went, He went with them. For many years I did not know what His purpose was in bringing them with Him all the time, but now we understand that His intention was to bring them all into His terminating death and into His germinating resurrection.

In addition, we need to realize that Peter, John, and James were the ones who were miserable, in darkness, under Satan's usurping hand, sick of fever, and contaminated by leprosy. It was Peter, John, and James who heard the gospel, who received the truth, and who were released from Satan's possession. These disciples were the ones who were healed of their fever, healed of the abnormal condition of their human life, and they were cleansed from leprosy. However, they were still deaf, dumb, and blind and thus they were still in need. When the time came, the Lord healed their ears. He thrust His fingers into their ears so that they could hear, healed their mouths so that they could speak, and especially the Lord opened their eyes so that they could see.

When the day of Pentecost came, we can see Peter standing there. He was the one who received the gospel, who saw the light of the truth, who was liberated from the possession of the usurper, who was healed from his abnormal situation and cleansed from his leprosy. His deaf ears were opened. Surely he heard God's word, his eyes saw the divine vision, and his mouth was opened wide to speak. As we have seen there was still something further. Finally, Peter was replaced. Peter as such a one was brought into Christ's death and into His resurrection. We may say that he became another person, a reproduction of Jesus, in the sense that something within him was conceived of the Holy Spirit with the divine essence, mingled with the human essence, yet terminated and germinated. In chapter one of Acts Peter was there as such a person. He was ready there for ten days. After those ten days the Holy Spirit that descended upon Jesus after His baptism descended again upon those people, and they were anointed. In a proper sense, just as we may say that Peter became a reproduction of Jesus, we may also say that they became Jesus. This is the ministry of the New Testament in the section of Jesus' ministry, along the line of Peter. Mark and the first twelve chapters of Acts are in the line of Peter.

If you consider this very Jesus who served God as a slave in such a ministry, what words could you use to describe this ministry? We have used a number of sentences to describe something of this ministry. I do believe that what has been spoken has created an impression within you that will cause you to see His ministry, which is the ministry of the New Testament.

In the Gospel of Luke

While this slave was serving to take care of God's household in this way, according to the Gospel of Luke, He was a genuine, perfect, and entire Man to seek and to save the lost sinners in the way of the highest standard of morality. It is very strange that certain cases are recorded only in Luke and not in the other Gospels. In Luke 7 there is the case of the son of the widow in Nain who was dead and being carried in a coffin on the street. The Lord Jesus came in to raise him up. Following this, there is the case of a sinful woman weeping and washing the feet of the Lord Jesus (Luke 7:37-38). In chapter ten there is the good Samaritan, and in chapter nineteen, Zaccheus, a chief tax collector.

All of these cases are found only in Luke, not in the other Gospels. If you consider these cases, you could realize that Jesus is presented here as a perfect Man who was carrying out His saving work in the highest standard of morality. Actually, the word morality is not adequate to describe His standard. The standard was something more excellent than morality, but we are short of words to describe it. Nevertheless, if you take this concept and go back to read the story of the good Samaritan, you could see something there that is not merely His saving, but His saving in a way that is indescribable.

It was against a very black background that the good Samaritan came to the wounded one in Luke 10. The Jews themselves called the Lord Jesus a Samaritan in John chapter eight (v. 48). Luke describes how a priest came to the place where the wounded one was, and he passed by on the opposite side of the road without doing anything.

Likewise, a Levite passed by and did not do anything. Then this good Samaritan, the despised One, came in a way that is beyond human words to describe. He was not asked or begged to do something to rescue the fallen one. He did everything out of Himself on His own initiative. Here is a story which shows us in what kind of standard and way, Jesus, the perfect Man, carried out His saving. This case does not emphasize His power. To call Lazarus out of the tomb shows His mighty divine power. However, this case shows us something of the highest standard of morality.

In the Gospel of Matthew

Then in Matthew this One lived a life that is the reality of the kingdom of the heavens. While He came as a Slave to serve God's household and as a Man to save the lost sinners in the highest standard of something that is beyond our utterance, this One lived a kingly life. Many Christian teachers talk about the kingdom in Matthew, but they have failed to see that the kingdom was portrayed by a kingly life which we do not have words to describe. This life portrays the reality of the kingdom of the heavens. If you want to know what the kingdom of the heavens is, you need to look at this life. In Matthew this life is the kingdom of the heavens.

In the Gospel of John

Furthermore, this matchless One who came as such a Slave, taking care of God's household, as such a perfect Man saving in that high standard, and as such a One who lived a life which was the kingdom of the heavens, also expressed God. God lived through Him, God was expressed through Him, He lived by God, and He lived as God. In the Gospel of John we see such a life as God's expression. What indescribable life is this? We must confess that we are utterly short of a proper vocabulary to describe such a fourfold life in this way. This life was the ministry of the Lord Jesus. You need to look at this ministry and also look at His Person. Consider what kind of Person He was and consider His ministry. This is marvelous. This is the New Testament ministry.

AN ALL-INCLUSIVE DEATH

After He had completed such a life as the very New Testament ministry, the Lord Jesus went to the cross to die a death as the last Adam (1 Cor. 15:45) to terminate the old man with the old creation. The death He died was also a death as the Lamb of God (John 1:29) to take away sin and its result—sins. In addition, He died a death as the brass serpent (John 3:14) to destroy Satan and his kingdom, the world. Moreover, we need to realize also that the Lord Jesus died to abolish the ordinances (Eph. 2:14-15) which include human culture, habits, and customs which divided the very mankind created by God. The death that He died to abolish all of these things may be designated the death of the Peacemaker. In addition, as a grain of wheat (John 12:24), He died a death which released the divine life. The Bible tells us that He died at least a fivefold death, a death as the last Adam, as the Lamb of God, as the brass serpent, as the Peacemaker, and as a grain of wheat. When He was dying there on the cross, in the eyes of God He was at least a fivefold Person, a Person in at least five aspects.

The Lord Jesus as such a Person terminated everything through such a death. That termination means that He accomplished the real baptism, as He said, "I have a baptism to be baptized with, and how I am pressed until it is accomplished!" (Luke 12:50). He had already been baptized, but He still had to go through a real baptism, a baptism that was the death on the cross, signified by the death water used by John the Baptist.

A NEW MAN AND A NEW CREATION IN RESURRECTION

On the positive side, through the death of the Lord Jesus, the divine life was released. In that divine life the very Jesus who had died was resurrected. Some of the things that were dealt with through His death could never come back again, including sin and sins, Satan and the world, and the ordinances, habits, and customs, but the old man and the old creation were resurrected. The Gospels of John and Luke do give us a sign concerning this matter. However, we need to realize that it is not easy to study the Bible properly and to understand it properly and adequately. On the morning of the resurrection, Mary and the other sisters and Peter and John went to the tomb. The man Jesus was gone, but the grave clothes were left there (John 20:5-7; Luke 24:12) representing all the things that were not related to the Person of the Lord Jesus. The old man and the old creation, however, were very much related to what the Lord Jesus was in His humanity. Therefore, that part was resurrected, but the rest that was buried was left in the tomb.

In the Life-study of Colossians we pointed out that God was busy when the Lord Jesus was dying on the cross (Message 23, p. 191). All the demons were busy, the evil angels were busy, and Satan was busy because it was not only Jesus that was crucified there on the cross. Jesus carried many things to the cross. He carried our sin and our sins, Satan and his world, and the ordinances, including the human culture, to the cross. Moreover, He carried the old man which was a part of His very being to the cross, and was related to the old creation. In His resurrection, though, He brought the old man and the old creation with Him.

For this reason, in God's germination there is the new man and the new heaven and the new earth. There is no such thing as a new Satan. There is no such thing as new sin or new ordinances. But out of the tomb there was brought forth a new man and a new creation! The rest was left in the tomb. On the morning of resurrection the disciples saw the grave clothes left in the tomb. Eventually, Mary the Magdalene saw this resurrected Man related to God's new creation.

THE LIFE-GIVING SPIRIT

In such a life Jesus became the life-giving Spirit. Now you can understand how He became the life-giving Spirit and also why He needed to become such a Spirit. Just as He needed to be incarnated to live a human life, in order that by this human life He could die to accomplish God's all-inclusive redemption, so also it was necessary at this time for Him to become such a life-giving Spirit.

All the old things were terminated at the cross of the Lord Jesus, and all the new things were germinated in His resurrection. Now in His resurrection He is the life-giving Spirit, and, as such a Spirit, He comes to germinate everyone chosen and predestinated by God according to Ephesians 1:4-5. He comes to germinate the chosen ones based upon His death and based upon His redemption, to make them the reproduction of Jesus in the same sense that Peter became another person, a reproduction of Jesus, in Acts 2. This is to produce the church, and this is the ministry of the New Testament in the section of the ministry of the Lord Jesus.

THE NEED TO SEE
THE INTRINSIC ESSENCE OF THE MINISTRY

In the case of messages such as these, we need much desperate prayer and fellowship that we might be brought into the depths of these truths and have the reality of them constituted into our very being. What I am sharing with you is what has been constituted into my own being over a period of many years. I am eager to pour out what has accumulated within me when there is opportunity. We hope to have a concluding training of the New Testament to review all these matters, but we expect that out of your prayer and exercise over these messages all of you would see something further concerning the New Testament ministry and something would be constituted within you. Among the majority of today's Christians, the concept of ministry is far short of what we are touching here, and their way of speaking about ministry is too superficial. If we mean business with the Lord, we should bear some part of the genuine ministry.

In this light concerning the New Testament ministry you could see where you should be, what you should be, and what you should do. As far as the ministry of the New Testament is concerned, you should not trust in your ability to speak, your ability to present doctrinal truth, your ability to write, or any of your other abilities. You should not think that you are qualified in those areas and therefore there is no problem with you. With some of you there is a definite problem. You should not think that any of your abilities qualify you for some part of the New Testament ministry. On that basis you are not qualified, for your abilities are not a part of the New Testament ministry and have nothing to do with the New Testament ministry.

Especially in the present situation I am very much burdened that we could see the intrinsic essence of God's New Testament ministry. I would caution the younger ones among us in particular that they have no standing to be proud of how much they know. There are some with us from the Far East who have been under my training for more than ten years; yet, from what I call the weather reports that have come to me, there are signs to indicate the danger of storms approaching. These weather reports have been the words that I have heard out of your own mouths. The same kind of weather reports have also come to me from different parts of this country in recent months. It was based on this pressing need that the decision was made to call these meetings for urgent fellowship to present these messages to you. Therefore, I would not consider this training an ordinary one, but rather something related to the urgent need. In these days we are very much in need of the Lord's mercy that we might see the very inner essence of the New Testament ministry. The Lord's recovery is much more than a matter of teaching the Bible, presenting doctrines, and even helping people to grow a little bit or holding conferences to edify others. All of these things are too superficial.

None of you have the standing to be proud of what you know. You may not realize how little you know, even how little has been wrought into you from the training we have had together. There are some among us who are off the track; whether you stay where you are or go to another place, you are off. Some of us have been in the Lord's recovery more than twenty years. There is the danger that we would become old and that we would become persons who feel that they are full. This is something of Laodicea. In some cases, these things may have happened already. What I have released to you is a small part of what is on my heart, a small portion to show you what God's New Testament ministry is.

A FIVEFOLD STANDARD

In carrying out God's New Testament ministry, the Lord Jesus told us that He never did anything out of Himself (John 5:19), He did not do His own work (John 4:34; 17:4), He did not speak His own word (John 14:10, 24), He did everything not by His own will (John 5:30), and He did not seek His own glory (John 7:18). If you use these few points as a standard to measure all the Christian work today, you can see that nearly all the Christian works fall short according to this yardstick. Who can say that they do not do anything in the Lord's work out of themselves? Who can say that they do not do their own work or speak their own words? Also, who can say that they do not do anything by their own will and that they do not do anything to seek their own glory? If we can answer these five points positively, I believe we are also in the New Testament ministry of God. If not, we are off.

This is the section of the Lord Jesus in God's New Testament ministry, and it is this that produces the church, edifies the saints, and builds up the Body. If you are short of these five points, whatever you do will be divisive and will cause division. Therefore, we need to see that there is a big difference with a terminated person who is not doing a work out of himself, not doing his own work, not speaking his own word, and who is not doing things by his own will and not seeking his own glory. This is not only a section of God's New Testament ministry, but our pattern, a pattern of such a Person with such a life. May the Lord make our vision clear concerning these matters.

CHAPTER FOUR

THE TRIUNE GOD FOR OUR EXPERIENCE

In the four Gospels the ministry of the New Testament began with John the Baptist. That was only a beginning, and the beginning of such a ministry was the termination of all the old things. That initial part of the ministry brought in the main section of the New Testament ministry, the ministry of Christ Himself.

We all have seen that Christ was One who was born of God and born with God to be a God-man. Even with Him there was a part that needed to be baptized, to be buried, to be terminated. That part was His humanity, and it was terminated and then resurrected. Therefore, He was a God-man with a humanity that had been terminated and resurrected. After His baptism, He was qualified and equipped to carry out the ministry of the New Testament; nevertheless, He needed the Spirit to come to descend upon Him. He was proper in every way, and He was properly anointed. Then He began the ministry.

As we have seen in the four Gospels, His part of the ministry was to bring people into the gospel, into the truth, into the liberation, into the healing, and into the cleansing. In addition, that part of the ministry healed people's deafness, dumbness, and blindness. Eventually, that part of the ministry brought all the saved ones into the terminating death of Christ and brought them into His germinating resurrection.

THE FATHER, THE SON, AND THE SPIRIT

After all His accomplishments in His earthly ministry,

the Lord Himself went to the cross to carry out the terminating death so that He could enter into the germinating resurrection. Here in this germinating resurrection He became the life-giving Spirit. This life-giving Spirit is the ultimate consummation of the Triune God in His relationship with us. All of us need to see this crucial point. The Triune God is the Father, the Son, and the Spirit. Until Christ entered into His resurrection and came back to the disciples in that germinating resurrection, there was no clear word in the Scriptures to reveal such a completed divine title, the Father, the Son, and the Spirit. Such a divine title is not found in the Old Testament. There are some hints in the Old Testament that indicate the Trinity of the Godhead with types, with figures, and with plain words, but it is not until Matthew 28:19 that the completed title, the Father, the Son, and the Spirit, is used for the first time.

We need to consider why it was that such a divine title was never revealed before the resurrection of Christ. The Trinity was not completely revealed because the Son with the Father had not completed the long process from incarnation, passing through His human life and His all-inclusive death, into the germinating resurrection. This long and very meaningful process needs much definition, according to a number of messages we have already given. Until the Lord Jesus had passed through death into resurrection, this long process was not completed.

DISTINCT BUT NOT SEPARATE

We need to be deeply impressed that the Son never did anything apart from the Father (John 5:19). Therefore, when He became something, He did that with the Father. This is a crucial point, and it is an intrinsic part of the meaning of Triune. The Son came in the Father's name (John 5:43), the Son came with the Father (John 6:46 and note 46[1]—Recovery Version), and the Son told us that the Father never left Him alone (John 8:29; 16:32). All the time the Father was with the Son, even in the Son's earthly life. The Son even told us while He was on this earth that He was in the Father and that the Father was in Him (John 10:38; 14:11; 17:21). This is the basis of what is called coinherence, which means living together in one another. You cannot separate the Son from the Father at all, and you should not try to make such a separation. The Father, Son, and Spirit are one God, not three Gods. Even to say three Persons is not quite correct. Griffith Thomas said that the word Persons may be borrowed because of the inadequacy of human language, but that it should not be pressed too far because it will lead to tritheism, the belief in three Gods.

We should be on guard concerning the inaccurate teaching of the so-called Trinity that stresses the matter of three separate Persons. It is permissible to use the word distinct in reference to the Three of the Trinity, but it is altogether inaccurate to use the word separate. This inaccurate teaching concerning three separate Persons of the Trinity has affected many Christians. This teaching is a part of the leaven in the prophecy of the Lord Jesus in Matthew 13:33. A woman took leaven and put it into the fine flour until the whole was leavened. According to the principles of chemistry, once leaven has been put into fine flour and mingled with it, the fine flour cannot be purified. This inaccurate teaching concerning the Trinity was the major part of the leaven that the Catholic Church put into the fine flour concerning Christ's Person. The truth of the Trinity has been leavened, but according to God Himself, one can never destroy or damage the truth. Nevertheless, according to our mentality, something has been damaged in relation to this truth. For over twenty-two years in this country I have been speaking again and again on this matter of the Trinity, and I am still very much burdened on this point. I fully realize that this thought concerning three Persons remains in all of you and even in me, unconsciously and subconsciously. A number of times I could not get through in certain passages of Scripture concerning the Trinity simply because these concepts still remain in me and work within me unconsciously and subconsciously. All of us were leavened in this matter of the Trinity.

THE SON WITH THE FATHER BECOMING THE SPIRIT

According to the basic principle, we all need to understand that the Son never did anything apart from the Father (John 5:19). Therefore, when the Son as the last Adam was going through the process of becoming the life-giving Spirit, He did not leave the Father on the throne and go through that process by Himself without the Father. Such a concept would be heretical. It is a basic principle that the Three have never been separated. From eternity past through time into eternity future the Three always coexist and coinhere. They have never been separated in any situation. In this principle, when the Bible says that the Son as the last Adam became a life-giving Spirit, it was the Son with the Father who became such a Spirit. Furthermore, this means that the Father within the Son became such a Spirit when the Son became the life-giving Spirit. These words may sound very new to you. This is the first time I have ever used these sentences, and I say these things with much consideration. To make such a statement is not a small thing, and I have been quite cautious in the past. However, after more than fifty years of study, after at least thirty years of consideration concerning how much I should release, I have the boldness at this point to say that when the Son as the last Adam became the life-giving Spirit, He did so in humanity with the Father. Therefore, the life-giving Spirit is the ultimate consummation of the Triune God in His relationship with us.

EXPERIENCING THE TRIUNE GOD

We need to see that the divine title, the Father, the Son,

and the Spirit, was revealed in a way that was for our experience, not for doctrine. Therefore, it is in His relationship with us that the life-giving Spirit is the ultimate consummation of the Triune God. Such a divine title was revealed in the Lord's word concerning the way to baptize people into the Trinity: "Go therefore and disciple all the nations, baptizing them into the name of the Father and of the Son and of the Holy Spirit" (Matt. 28:19). This divine title is revealed in a way that is for our experience, not in a way of doctrine for us to study. We are not learning the Triune God, but experiencing Him. I would make a strong declaration that we cannot understand the Triune God, but we thank the Lord that we are all qualified to experience Him.

You may think it sounds quite strange to say that we cannot understand the Triune God, but we can experience Him. However, no one would claim to understand the food we eat every day, not even the doctors or the dietitians. Who understands an egg, a glass of milk, or a slice of bread? Even the experts in nutrition have a certain understanding at one time and a very different concept at another time as a result of further studies. If we cannot understand the food we eat to nourish our bodies, how can we expect to understand the Triune God who is life to us, the One who is the bread of life to us (John 6:35), and the One who said, "He who eats Me shall also live because of Me" (John 6:57)? We may not know, and we cannot understand, but we can eat, and we can enjoy. I enjoy the Triune God every day. I do not say that I understand Him, but I certainly enjoy Him.

TWO MYSTERIES: DISTINCTION AND ONENESS

There are two mysteries in the Triune Godhead which no one can explain. The distinction between the Father, the Son, and the Spirit is one mystery which no one can define or explain. The oneness among the Three is the second mystery; otherwise, there could not be one God. The

Three are one; three denotes distinction, and one denotes the oneness. No matter how much you study this matter or how much you get into the research of the theological writings, the issue of your study of this matter will consummate in these two mysteries, the mystery of the distinction of the Three, and the mystery of the oneness of the Godhead among the Three. It is impossible for any human mentality to understand these two mysteries or to explain them. I have tried over and over, but there is no way. I have been doing this work for more than thirty years, but all I can tell you is that there are these two points, these two mysteries—the distinction and the oneness.

While we say that the Lord is the Father and that He is also the Spirit, we cannot annul the distinction between them. To do so would be heretical. From the black and white in the pages of the Bible, you can tell that there is a distinction between the Three. Even the way of expression denotes some distinction. The Lord Jesus said, "I am in the Father, and the Father is in Me" (John 14:10). It sounds like They are one, but there is a distinction. If there were no distinction, the Lord Jesus would not have made such a statement, nor would He have used the divine title, the Father, the Son, and the Spirit in Matthew 28:19. No one can explain the fact that there are three expressions and that these expressions denote a distinction. Nevertheless, the best Bible teachers all agree that these Three are only one name. In Matthew 28:19 the Lord Jesus used the name in the singular, "Baptizing them into the name." This name indicates the oneness.

We cannot explain the fact that there is a distinction and there is the oneness, but we can experience the Trinity day by day. When we enjoy the Lord, we enjoy the Father, and we enjoy the Spirit. When we say, "O Lord," the Spirit is here, and the Father is here also. By this you can see in principle that when the Lord Jesus as the Son in His humanity, the last Adam, became the life-giving Spirit, He did so with the Father. Therefore, when the Son passed through His human death and entered into resurrection to become the life-giving Spirit, He did it with the Father. It was not the case that the Son alone became the life-giving Spirit without the Father; rather, it was the Son with the Father who passed through the process to become the life-giving Spirit. In resurrection the Son with the Father became the life-giving Spirit, the ultimate consummation of the Triune God. Now, when you touch the life-giving Spirit, you touch also the Son and the Father.

THE ALL-INCLUSIVE ANOINTING

It was when the Apostle John touched the matter of the anointing that he said that if you deny that Jesus is the Christ, you deny both the Son and the Father; everyone who denies the Son does not have the Father either; he who confesses the Son has the Father also (1 John 2:20, 22-23). If we spend time in these verses and get into the depths of the truth here, we could realize that Jesus, Christ, the Son, and the Father are all the ingredients of the all-inclusive anointing in 1 John 2.

We may use an all-inclusive health drink as an illustration of the anointing in 1 John 2. In one drink there may be milk, fruit, protein, and perhaps some vitamins and other ingredients. When you take one sip of this drink, you have all of the ingredients that are in it. In a similar way, when you touch the all-inclusive anointing in 1 John 2, you touch Jesus, you touch Christ, you touch the Son, you touch the Father, and you even touch the eternal life (1 John 2:25). These five elements of the divine anointing are clearly mentioned in this chapter—Jesus, Christ, the Son, the Father, and the eternal life. They can be compared to five spices or five ingredients for the compounding of such an all-inclusive anointing. By the anointing of the all-inclusive, compound Spirit, who is the composition of the divine Trinity, we know and enjoy the Father, the Son, and the Spirit as our life and life supply.

CHAPTER FIVE

THE CONTINUATION
OF THE NEW TESTAMENT MINISTRY
WITH PETER AND PAUL IN THE ACTS

THE LORD BREATHING HIMSELF INTO THE DISCIPLES

After such a long process from incarnation through resurrection, a process in which He carried out the ministry of the New Testament and set the pattern for the New Testament ministry, the Lord Jesus became the very consummation of the Triune God, the life-giving Spirit. Then in the night of His resurrection He came back to His disciples not to teach them, not to carry out some work, but to breathe into them (John 20:22). He breathed this ultimate consummation of the Triune God into Peter and all the others. The Lord came not only with the life-giving Spirit but as the life-giving Spirit, as the all-inclusive, ultimate consummation of the Triune God, to do one thing—to breathe Himself into the disciples. Such a breathing into them was sufficient for their spiritual life.

A NEW PETER

It is very interesting that after this breathing in John 20 He did something further in the next chapter, in John 21. The very next chapter in the Bible after John 21 is Acts 1. In Acts 1 and 2 we see another Peter, a different Peter. He is not the same one who was there in the four Gospels. Here is a Peter who has been transformed and even replaced in full. If you were an uneducated person from a primitive culture, one who had no knowledge of Christianity, and then you were saved and began to read the Bible for the first time, you would be shocked when you came to the opening pages of Acts. In reading the four Gospels, you would have an impression of Peter as one who was a natural man and an uneducated fisherman, always behaving in a natural way. However, the Peter in the opening pages of Acts is strikingly different. He understood the Bible and knew how to interpret it. He had not graduated from any seminary, nor did he have any education in theology or any theological degree. Nevertheless, this fisherman became a person who knew the Bible, and he took the lead to remain in Jerusalem for ten days in spite of the threatening of the Jews. He no longer cared for his fishing; he did not care for anything except the prayer in that upper room. He took the lead to remain there to pray with the one hundred twenty for ten days. How could the Peter in the Gospels do such a thing? Even consider yourself—do you think you could remain together in oneness with one hundred twenty others to pray for ten days?

Only a short time before, the disciples had been fighting among themselves. All the others became indignant because James and John wanted to be at the right hand and left hand of the King (Matt. 20:20-28; Mark 10:35-45). Now in chapter one of Acts those who had been fighting among themselves were together in unity, in oneness, with a pure intention and a purified desire. Right after the Lord's death and resurrection, they all became different persons because the life-giving Spirit as the ultimate consummation of the Triune God had been breathed into their being. In that unique, all-inclusive drink they received everything; they received the Triune God, and they also received the uplifted humanity, the proper human living, the terminating death, and the germinating resurrection.

In medical science, the greatest thing is to know how to

inject all the necessary elements into the human body. Compared to this, surgery is not so wonderful. We should not compare God to a surgeon, but rather we should recognize Him as the wonderful One who injects Himself as the all-inclusive nourishment into our being. It was because of such a life-giving injection that we can say Peter was another person in the first two chapters of Acts.

ONE HUNDRED TWENTY IN ONENESS

Not only Peter, or even only two or three others, but also all the other one hundred twenty were changed. One hundred twenty men and women, all Galileans, who were despised by the local people, were remaining in Jerusalem in one accord not for any entertainment or amusement, but only to pray to One they could not see. There was nothing for their eyes to see, there was no outward attraction, and there was certainly no entertainment. They remained there under the threatening for ten days, praying in one accord.

We need to consider what could make it possible for those one hundred twenty to remain in oneness. What had happened to change the situation so much in such a short time? The very element of Jesus had been injected into their being so they were the reproduction, the continuation, the increase of Jesus. Whatever had been there as an ingredient in Jesus in the four Gospels was injected into the one hundred twenty in Acts 1. The first chapter of Acts is a continuation of the record of Jesus after His baptism, after the crucifixion. After Jesus was baptized in the Jordan, He was ready to be anointed, and He was anointed (John 1:32). Now, in Acts 1, the one hundred twenty were also ready to be anointed. In a sense, they were no longer natural, and they were no longer living in the old man, in the old creation. There is no need to say that they were no longer living in sin or in the world. They had been replaced with this wonderful Jesus through His death and resurrection, and they were, therefore, ready to be anointed. When the day of Pentecost came, the Spirit descended upon them economically just as the Spirit had descended upon Jesus after His baptism. Therefore, from Acts 2 Peter took the lead to stand up with at least eleven others to carry out the New Testament ministry that John had initiated and Jesus had continued. Their ministry was a continuation of the ministry of the Lord Jesus.

PETER'S CONTINUATION OF THE MINISTRY OF THE LORD JESUS

The five times that Peter stood up to speak are recorded in Acts, in chapters two, three, four, five, and ten. Four times he spoke to the Jews, and the fifth time to the Gentiles. If we consider what he spoke on those five occasions, we can see that he did not teach theology, philosophy, morality, ethics, human behavior, human character, science, or psychology. His speaking had nothing at all to do with any of these things. Rather he spoke concerning the incarnation of Jesus and His human living. When he said that God had raised up One out of the descendants of David, he was speaking concerning the incarnation (Acts 2:29-30). When he told us that God anointed Jesus and that He worked and traveled through all the places, he was speaking concerning the human living of Jesus (Acts 10:38). It is the same when he told us that Jesus preached the gospel, healed the sick, and released the ones oppressed by Satan, as recorded in the Gospels. He had been crucified by those who were now listening to Peter, but God raised Him up, because death could not hold Him (Acts 2:24; 3:15; 4:10; 5:30; 10:40). Furthermore, God exalted Him to the throne, making Him the Lord and the Christ (Acts 2:32-36; 5:31). In addition, Peter said that the Lord Jesus became the cornerstone of God's building, which is the church. In the beginning of Peter's ministry in chapters two, three, and four of Acts the church is not mentioned, but the church is indicated in his reference to the stone for God's building in 4:11. (The best manuscripts do not have the word church in Acts 2:47, as found in the King James Version.)

From these points we can see that Peter's ministry was simply a continuation and a repetition of the ministry of Jesus. When Peter preached the gospel, he did not use illustrations and parables as we often do. The reason we need to use parables and illustrations is that we are short of the resurrection life and short of the Spirit's power. Due to this shortage, our poverty compels us to pick up parables from different sources. If we are saturated with the resurrection life, even soaked in it, and if we are clothed with power from on high, we have no need for such parables. Rather, it will be sufficient simply to point out the facts to the people. This was exactly what Peter did. His preaching did not distract anyone; it was frank, direct, and very much to the point. He told the people that Jesus was raised up out of the seed of David, He was anointed, He worked, He preached the gospel, and He released the ones who were oppressed. They rejected Him and put Him to death by crucifying Him, but death could not hold Him. God raised Him up and exalted Him to the throne, and He made Him the Lord and the Christ.

In this light we need to check our own so-called ministry. We have to confess that our ministry is not so pure and that there are many distracting elements in it. In a pure way, without any distractions, Peter referred to the Old Testament, but he did not expound any part of it. He was not teaching the Bible or holding a Bible study class, because he did not need to do that. Peter was a person replaced by Christ and with Christ, and he was empowered with the Spirit from on high.

We need to spend time to consider carefully those five messages of Peter to see what kind of ministry Peter was carrying out. Actually, it was the same ministry which was carried out in the four Gospels, even an extract of the four Gospels. Just as the church was mentioned in the section of Christ's ministry in the four Gospels, the church was also indicated in the section of Peter's ministry. The mention of the church in the Gospels indicated that the ministry of Jesus would lead to the producing of the church, and Peter indicated the same thing when he said that God had raised up and exalted the very One whom they had rejected to the throne, and that this One had become the cornerstone of God's building for the church to be built up.

THE MINISTRY OF PAUL

Of course, the ministry of Peter was not the ministry for the producing and building up of the church in full. Such a church-producing and church-building ministry came in with the Apostle Paul. After the first twelve chapters of Acts, the ministry of Paul is initiated in Acts 13. Acts 14 tells us that Paul preached the gospel to many people in many cities, and that he came back to visit them and to establish elders in every church (v. 23). From this we can see that the ministry of Paul was more than a continuation of the ministry of John the Baptist, the ministry of Jesus Christ, and the ministry of Peter. Paul's ministry went on from the incarnation of Christ, His human living, His all-inclusive, terminating death, His germinating resurrection, and His ascension to the producing and the building up of the Body of Christ.

Before Paul's ministry, the church was not revealed in full in the New Testament. There was some indication in the word of the Lord Jesus and then in the word of Peter, but the matter of the church began to be fully covered when Paul came into the New Testament ministry. Therefore, in the sixteen chapters from chapter thirteen to chapter twenty-eight of Acts, Paul repeated the ministry of John the Baptist, of Jesus, and of Peter in a number of messages that he gave, but there was also something further in his part of the New Testament ministry.

Three Problems

In Paul's time, in his part of the ministry, there were three problems: the problem of the Gentile churches, the problem of handling the relationship between the Gentile churches and the Jewish churches, and the problem of the so-called co-workers. None of these problems were there in the section of Peter's ministry. Peter was appointed and designated directly and officially by the Lord Jesus. No one could deny his authentic authority. In that time the work was under Peter's leadership.

However, at the time of Paul's appointment, he himself was the only one who saw the heavenly vision (Acts 26:13-19). Such a situation compelled the Lord to send a brother named Ananias to confirm him (Acts 9:10-17). We may think it would have been wonderful if the Lord had sent Peter to confirm Paul, but instead the Lord sent a brother who is mentioned in the Bible only in connection with this one thing (Acts 9:10-17; 22:12-16). Although the Bible says that Ananias had a good report of all the Jews there, it is strange that he is not mentioned any other time. It seems that no one knew this brother, and that he was good to be used in the Lord's hand only to do this one thing—to confirm Paul when he came to Damascus.

Some may have questioned Paul in a critical way saying, "You, Saul of Tarsus, who do you think you are? Do you really think that you have been appointed by the Lord to be an apostle? When Stephen was being stoned to death, you were there helping those stoning him. Do you really expect us to believe that now you have become an apostle, and not only an apostle, but the one to take the lead in the Lord's work? Do you think Apollos should be under you, and even Barnabas should be under you? It was Barnabas that brought you in. Therefore, Barnabas must be above you, and you must be under Barnabas. Apollos knows the Bible, and he knows how to present the Bible in a very attractive way. Saul, how much of the Bible can you expound? Who do you think you are that you should take the lead?"

No doubt there was a problem among the so-called co-workers. Barnabas disagreed with Paul, even though he was the one who had brought him in (Acts 9:27; 15:36-40). We can see the indications of the problems not only with Paul and Barnabas, but even the more between Paul and Peter. No one can deny that Paul and Peter were co-workers, but there was, nevertheless, something not so smooth or sweet in their relationship. Paul says in Galatians 2 that God appointed Peter and also John and James as apostles to the Jews, and God appointed him as an apostle to the Gentiles (vv. 7-9). There is a strong indication of the problem between these co-workers in the same chapter where Paul tells us that he rebuked Peter to his face (v. 11). In addition, Paul tells us in 1 Corinthians that there was a problem when some were saying that they were of Cephas, and some were saying that they were of Paul. Paul suffered because of this problem.

Moreover, if Paul had received a vision to go back to Jerusalem to strengthen Peter and James and to establish churches in Judea among the Jews, God's chosen people, that would have been easy for him to do. We need to consider, though, what it meant for Paul to receive a commission to go to the Gentile world to establish the Gentile churches. It was very hard for Peter even to go to visit a Gentile family within the territory of the Jewish land. It was hard for Peter to get even a little out of the atmosphere of the Jews. Now here was another one, a typical Jew, who received a commission to go into the Gentile world to establish Gentile churches. We should not think it was easy for Paul to carry out his commission.

Eventually, trouble came to the Gentile churches from the source of the Judaizers who came to Antioch, the source of the Gentile churches. There was a conflict in Antioch that forced Paul to go to Jerusalem; he had no choice. From the account of the conference in Jerusalem in Acts 15, we can see how much Paul had learned. I do not believe that the decision made there under the leadership of James was satisfactory to Paul (Acts 15:19-21, 28-29). Paul could not have been satisfied with that decision, but he tolerated it. Otherwise, he would have told the brothers in Jerusalem strongly that they should make the definite decision to forget about the law and not to mention it again. Nevertheless, the very Paul who rebuked Peter strongly regarding the matter of law (Gal. 2:11-16), tolerated the outcome of that conference in Jerusalem. Now you can see that there was a problem between the Gentile churches established by Paul and the Jewish churches established by Peter. That problem was not a small thing. Therefore, Paul was forced to tolerate a neutral, "grey" decision. There was no absoluteness in that decision, but rather a compromise.

Entangled in the Old Net

That decision in Acts 15 with its element of compromise produced Acts 21. In the last visit paid by Paul to Jerusalem, it is as if "the tail of the fox" came out. James took the lead to tell Paul to look at the tens of thousands of Jewish believers, all zealous for the law (v. 20). They were even practicing the Nazarite vow of the Old Testament. At that very time, four were there taking such a vow, but they were poor and unable to pay the price for the sacrifices, the offerings. James advised Paul to pay the charges for them so that he could share in their vow. In this way Paul was dragged into the old net, the very net that he himself had torn into pieces in Romans and Galatians. In those two writings Paul had torn the old net of Judaism into pieces to the uttermost. However, that net was still in existence in Jerusalem, and when he went there, it seemed that he entered into the net and was caught.

In that situation Paul was nice, unimposing, and tolerant. He may have thought to himself, "I wrote the Epistle to the Romans, and I wrote the Epistle to the Galatians, but I also wrote 1 Corinthians chapter nine, 'To the Jews I became as a Jew' (v. 20). Now it must be the time for me to be a Jew." At any rate, he tolerated that situation in Acts 21, and he participated in that Old Testament vow. This was serious. This would damage God's economy in the New Testament to the uttermost. Therefore, on the last day of the vow the Lord came in. It was as if the Lord told Paul that he may have tolerated that situation, but the Lord Himself would never tolerate it. Therefore, the Lord brought the whole thing to an end. The vow was not completed, and Paul was arrested. This was the ending of that part of Paul's ministry.

A Clear Sky in Prison

You may say that Paul ministered in another way after that time, but at the very least you must admit that the first part of his ministry was ended by his mistake. Then the Lord kept him in prison away from any kind of frustration, attraction, distraction, and influence. He was isolated from everything in prison and the sky was clear.

Under that clear sky in the prison Paul wrote the Epistles to the Ephesians, to the Philippians, and to the Colossians. After his first imprisonment he wrote 1 Timothy and Hebrews, and during his second imprisonment he wrote 2 Timothy. Most Bible teachers recognize that these books are high, deep, and profound, and that they touch the very heart of God's New Testament economy. How could Paul write in such a way? He could do it because he was under a clear sky with a clear view to look at God's economy. If that vow in Acts 21 had been completed and Paul had still been free to continue his travels, his ministry would have become the carrying out of a mixture. In that case, the entire history of the Acts would have been changed.

We all need to be deeply impressed with the significance of Acts 21—even such a strong apostle as the Apostle Paul, one with a clear view of God's economy, was not that strong in facing the problem in Jerusalem and not that accurate in his action in that kind of situation. If Paul had been stronger and more accurate in facing the problem in Jerusalem, he would have told James that he absolutely would never agree to participate in that Old Testament vow. Rather, he would have urged James to cancel that vow, take those four brothers out from under the vow, and forget about the temple. He may have said, "Brother James, I am sorry that I could never take your word. Why would you go back to offer the cattle as sacrifices again? Do you not know that the offerings of the cattle were in the old dispensation, and that was fulfilled by the Lord Jesus? When He came, He offered Himself once to replace all the offerings. Why would we go back to offer the old dispensation offerings again? To do such a thing is an insult to the Lord Jesus in the heavens. If you brothers in Jerusalem and in Judea would still go back to the old Judaic religion, that is your decision, but please do not try to convince me. I am sorry, brother, but I would never go back to that old way." If Paul had done this, I do not believe he would have been put into prison. Then he would have been able to go on to take another journey for his ministry, perhaps to Spain as he had planned (Rom. 15:28). His journeys for the ministry were ended by his mistake. The Lord put him into prison in order to clear up the cloudy sky.

Not many years later, God sent an army under Titus to destroy all of Jerusalem to clear up the situation. It was as if God said to forget about Jerusalem and about the tens of thousands of believers zealous for the law. The Lord cleared up the situation that was clouded by the mixture of the old things of Judaism with the New Testament economy. This is history, and no one can deny the facts of history.

What was left after Jerusalem was destroyed were some deeper Epistles written by the Apostle Paul under a clear sky. The cloud of mixture was blown away, and the apostle who tolerated too much was disciplined to be very clear concerning God's economy. Therefore, he wrote these deeper Epistles, which have all become the most rich inheritance to us today.

We need to consider what would have happened if Paul had succeeded in his way of being tolerant and that vow of the Nazarite had been completed. Suppose that had been the case, and suppose Paul had left Jerusalem after the seventh day of that vow with the best wishes of the Jewish brothers for a good journey, and he continued on in that way. Suppose Jerusalem had never been destroyed, but still remained today with the church full of its mixture of Judaism as it was then, and suppose Ephesians, Philippians, Colossians, 1 Timothy, Hebrews, and 2 Timothy had never been written. We need to consider seriously what the situation would be today if that had been the case.

Today's Christianity is altogether in a clouded situation even after God's stern dealings with the church of mixture in A.D. 70 to clear up that situation. If there had not been such a clearing up carried out by God to put Paul into prison, to destroy Jerusalem, and to use Paul to write these few deeper Epistles, including Ephesians, Philippians, Colossians, 1 Timothy, Hebrews, and 2 Timothy, we would be in a clouded situation today. How we thank the Lord that these three things are facts in history, and we are inheriting these facts as our rich portion. With such a rich inheritance as our portion, we should no longer be in a situation that is clouded by the mixture of Judaism.

THE UNIQUE MINISTRY OF THE NEW TESTAMENT

It is not the purpose of the New Testament ministry to carry out anything other than the incarnation of the Triune God, His human living, His all-inclusive terminating death, His germinating resurrection, and His exalting ascension to replace God's chosen people with such a One so that the members of Christ could be produced to form a Body as the expression of the Triune God. This is the ministry of the New Testament. It has nothing to do with theology, philosophy, morality, ethics, culture, or religion.

It is only related to this wonderful Person, to His life, and to His ministry to produce the believers as members to form the Body of Christ. We need to be deeply impressed with this point.

None of us should put out anything to satisfy people's curiosity or to show that we know something more than others or that we know something new. The Gnostics knew many things that were strange. The Judaizers preached things that were different from the things the apostles preached. Through the twenty centuries what has been put out has been one new thing after another, different from the teachings of others.

Some would say that they do not like to follow Paul in their preaching. They would rather preach something new and different. Actually, their preaching does not contain anything new; it is only different. There are some who think that it is a shame to preach, to teach, to speak, or to write the same things that others have. They expect to receive a special glory for themselves by speaking and teaching something different to show that they know something others do not know. All of these attitudes are a shame.

Moreover, dear saints, we need to see that all of these things could be under the cloak that they are for the defending of the truth, for the defending of the faith, or for the further recovery of the biblical truth. Nevertheless, we need to realize that the issue of this kind of teaching has always been a division. Every denomination, every division, and every free group is based upon a certain so-called truth other than the New Testament ministry. To be a Presbyterian means to take the presbytery as the ground to build a Presbyterian denomination. To baptize people by immersion has been taken as a base to form the Baptist denomination. These items are not the basic and central elements of the New Testament ministry.

We all need to be very clear what the New Testament ministry is. The ministry of John the Baptist initiated the

ministry of Christ, and the ministry of Peter continued
Christ's ministry. Paul's ministry continued and further
developed all the foregoing ministry and went forward to
reach the goal to build up the Body of Christ. This is the
New Testament ministry.

However, if you look at today's situation, you will
realize that there are many different ministries in addition
to this unique New Testament ministry. If you could take
away all the different ministries and leave only the unique
ministry of the New Testament, all the denominations, all
the different groups, and all the divisions, would disappear.
There would be no division and no confusion.

All of us need to learn this sober lesson and be on the
alert not to deviate from the ministry of the New
Testament. If we carry out something new, something
different, something other than this unique ministry, we
will be through as far as the Lord's recovery is concerned.
Actually, the Lord's recovery is to bring us back to the
unique ministry of the New Testament.

CHAPTER SIX

THE CONTINUATION AND FURTHER DEVELOPMENT IN PAUL'S PART OF THE NEW TESTAMENT MINISTRY

Of the twenty-seven books of the New Testament, Paul has written fourteen. Therefore, we may say that Paul's Epistles occupy more than half of the books of the New Testament. In this chapter we need to see Paul's part in the New Testament ministry from his fourteen Epistles.

No doubt Paul has covered many, many items in his fourteen Epistles. For this reason, it is easy for us to lose our direction when we begin to get into them, somewhat like a person who loses his direction going into a forest. I would particularly encourage the young brothers to spend much more time in reading Paul's writings, if you mean business to get into their depths. You need to put aside your knowledge, your understanding of theology, philosophy, culture, religion, ethics, and morality and come to these fourteen books with a clear mind, even a clarified mind, and an emptied spirit, with a pure heart. Otherwise, you cannot get into what Paul has written. Furthermore, you need to read through the fourteen Epistles more than ten times. Do not read them all at one time but perhaps once or twice during this week, then again after a month, and continue in this way throughout a year's time. As you are reading, you need to pick up the crucial points and to recall what you have seen through the Life-studies. If you put aside all your knowledge to empty yourself, clarify your mind, and purify your heart to read in this way, I believe you will see something.

CHRIST AND THE CHURCH

After many years of study in this line, I can tell you that Paul's part of the ministry of the New Testament is altogether not different from the part of the Lord Jesus. The only thing that constitutes a difference at all is that in Paul's part the ministry has gone on. In fact, it has gone on very much from Christ to the church. You need to keep this one crucial point in mind in all your reading, that Paul's fourteen books are on Christ and the church.

A number of years ago in Taiwan we began to use some slogans concerning Christ and the church: "We are for Christ and the church," and, "The great mystery is Christ and the church." Expressions like these are still being used among many of you dear ones from the Far East, but according to my observation, you failed to go on further to study all the aspects concerning Christ. You used these slogans, but you did not dig into their meaning. Regretfully, it seems that you have taken the easy way. When you go out to preach and when you teach, minister, or pray, you carry out all these things according to what you have already learned. I am afraid that you are like a high school graduate who refuses to go further into the sphere of a university, or like a university graduate who refuses to go on into the realm of graduate study. Instead, you remain where you are and use all the things that you received long ago. Therefore, it is hard for people to see any improvement in your understanding of Christ in different aspects or in your understanding concerning the church.

THE NEED FOR CONTINUAL IMPROVEMENT

In your understanding concerning Christ and the church, you have received a certain amount. You merely keep what you have and use what you have, but there is no progress, no improvement. In such a case, it is always easy not only for your listeners to lose interest but also for you yourself because there is no freshness. Some of you are teaching the things concerning Christ still in about the same way, with the same points, and the same aspects, as we were teaching thirty years ago.

Suppose you are learning something further concerning mathematics above the university level in graduate school. As a graduate student in mathematics, your presentation to the elementary students is very interesting to them. You are able to teach in a very elementary way with rich points that attract people. Your teaching is much different from that of a high school graduate who is learning mathematics and trying to teach mathematics in the elementary school with a teaching that always causes everyone to lose interest.

THE INCARNATION OF CHRIST IN PAUL'S WRITINGS

Now we come to Paul's teachings concerning Christ. I would like to give you some direction to help you get into Paul's teachings concerning Christ and the church. You need much study after you have read the fourteen Epistles at least ten times.

After you have finished the reading, you need to take a subject such as the incarnation of Christ and study this matter in Paul's writings. At this point in your study, you should not go to other books, but pick up all the verses directly or indirectly related to this point in Paul's writings. Then you need to put all the verses concerning the incarnation of Christ together and pray—undoubtedly you will see something there.

If you take this way to get into Paul's writings, I believe you will see much. For example, very few readers pay attention to the opening word of Paul in the book of Romans. First he tells us that what he is going to write is the gospel of God, which was spoken by the prophets in the past, concerning His Son. From this point, he goes on to tell us that according to the flesh, Jesus Christ is out of the seed of David, but according to the Spirit of holiness, He has been designated the Son of God (Rom. 1:1-4). Here the

Person of Christ is very much described, not just revealed. Therefore, here is a verse with at least one point that indicates Christ's incarnation. To say that Christ came out of the seed of David according to the flesh is directly related to His incarnation. Nevertheless, I doubt that many of you have ever paid attention to this point in reading Romans because you have been possessed with the concept that Romans is concerning sin, concerning God's condemnation, or concerning God's justification, sanctification, and transformation.

In the opening word of Romans, however, the Apostle Paul does not tell us that the gospel is concerning these matters. He stresses that the gospel of God is concerning God's Son, the One according to two elements—according to the flesh and according to the Spirit. Some of you may have read this book a number of times, but I doubt that you have paid your full attention to this point. I am afraid that you know a lot, but you neglect the Person of Christ.

ON THE CENTRAL LINE WITH NO DISTRACTIONS

Here we have some of the elements, some of the intrinsic essences, in Paul's part of the New Testament ministry. These are crucial points. There is no need to look for some new thought or to pick up some peculiar point to present a message different from mine. Rather, you need to develop the knowledge concerning Christ being the Son of God and the One out of the seed of David according to the flesh, and you need to give messages on these matters. There is no need for you to follow me; I am not interested in that. What I want to see is that whatever you put out is absolutely in the basic elements, the intrinsic essences, of the New Testament ministry. I hope that all of you could develop more messages than what I have ever given along this line. Such a thing would be wonderful.

Of course, I would be deeply troubled if any of you would pick up some peculiar point, some strange thought, thus clouding a message to distract people from the central line, even from the focus of God's New Testament ministry. I would hate to see any of you do such a thing. If my vision is keen, surely it is keen in this line to detect things of this nature. Just by reading a few lines of what you have written, without reading an entire article, I can tell whether or not you are off in this matter. I do not expect you merely to repeat the messages I have given. Rather, I would hope that you could receive help from my messages and stand on my shoulders to go on further to present more things. Then I would come to you to learn of you, and I would stand on your shoulders to see something even further.

I have encouraged nearly all of you to study Greek, especially the young ones. But it was not my intention that you get into such a study to dig out some peculiar points or some strange thoughts. That is a wrong concept. It is necessary for you to keep yourself in the line and focus of the New Testament ministry. What Brother Watchman Nee and I have done is simply to lay a good foundation for the Lord's recovery for you to stand on to go further to build upon it. We do not like to see you set something else as another foundation.

THE UNIQUE FOUNDATION—
CHRIST FOR THE BUILDING UP OF THE CHURCH—
AND THE PROPER BUILDING MATERIALS

Paul told us clearly that he had laid the foundation, as a wise master builder (1 Cor. 3:10-11). He has laid the unique foundation, and no one can lay another. He warned us and cautioned us not to lay another foundation, but he encouraged us to build upon the foundation he had laid. Furthermore, he told us that we need to be careful, to take heed, how we build upon the foundation. Surely Paul did not like to see foundations laid other than the unique foundation he had already laid, nor did he like to see wood, hay, and stubble used for the building up. What we like to see is more gold, more silver, and more precious stones built upon the unique foundation. I would strongly encourage all of you brothers to continue to build. Certainly I am not jealous concerning what you may be able to do; rather, I am very much expecting to see that all of you can go further.

Nevertheless, I say again that I surely would not be happy to see any of you put out something as a foundation other than the unique foundation. Among Christians one foundation after another has been put out through the years, which are all different from the unique foundation, and different foundations are continuing to be put out. One put out the presbytery as a foundation, another put out baptism by immersion, a third put out episcopalianism, that is controlling people by the bishops, another put out tongue-speaking, and yet another put out holiness as a foundation. There are many different foundations which are all different from the unique foundation.

In such a situation we all need to be very clear that the unique foundation for the building up of the church in the New Testament ministry is Christ. There is no other foundation. Once you are clear concerning this point, you need to consider carefully what you should do. You need to keep yourself preserved all the time in this narrow field, in the field of Christ for the church. You need to do your work in the field or sphere of Christ for the church with care lest you get out of this sphere.

When I encourage you to keep yourself within the sphere of Christ for the church, I do not mean that you should not use the books of other writers for help. However, if you do not have a solid foundation laid, you may be distracted when you go to their books. It may seem that they lead you into some forest. Therefore, I hope that all of you, especially the young saints among us, will have a good foundation laid through reading and studying the Life-studies. Surely the

Life-studies will help you to lay a good foundation with adequate discernment.

With such a solid foundation, I encourage you to go to some of the books of other writers. I myself use a number of books in my study and preparation for writing the notes for the Recovery Versions. When I am working with my helpers, you might find anywhere from ten to twenty or more books open on my desk while we are working. However, in using all these books, it is necessary to have the proper discernment. In a good number of cases, the first part of a sentence may be very good, but the last part is off. It is not always easy to exercise adequate discernment. Therefore, I would encourage you to take care of the matter of laying a good foundation, and then exercise yourself to be careful when you go to the books of other writers.

THE HUMAN LIVING OF CHRIST AS REVEALED BY PAUL

Suppose you have already taken this way to study the incarnation of Christ in the writings of Paul; you have already spent time to pick up all the verses related to this point, and have put them together with much prayer. The second point for your study is the human life of Christ in Paul's books. If you study in this way, when someone brings up the matter of the human life of Christ, you will immediately have a good collection of all the points in Paul's books. If you were asked, you could give these points without thinking. For example, you might make reference to the aspects of Christ's human life on this earth unveiled in Philippians 2:5-8. Not only the four Gospels but also the writings of Paul unveil to us the human living of Christ.

Actually, it would be hard for you to understand what is narrated in the four Gospels without Paul's interpretation. It would not be so easy for us to understand that the life portrayed in the Gospel of Mark is the living of a slave without Paul's word in Philippians 2 telling us that the human living of Christ is the living of a slave. Here is an indication that Paul's ministry was not one of setting up new things or strange things, but it was rather a ministry of developing what had been set up already. A portrait had been set up in Mark, but it needed some interpretation, some development, of the definition of that portrait. This is the way for you to get into these matters.

ONE FIELD AND ONE MAJOR
WITH RICHER AND RICHER DEVELOPMENT

What there is for you to develop is as large as the ocean. Brother Nee and I have done only a little. There is no need for you to get into another field. To do that would be to take the wrong way. The Lord's recovery cannot be compared to a university with many different schools and many different majors. Rather, the Lord's recovery is like a unique school with one field and only one major, and the major is Christ for the church. In the Lord's recovery there are no other majors, and all of us need to concentrate our study in this one major.

You should not consider that you prefer to say something new and to open another school in the Lord's recovery with something different from what was set up by Brother Nee and followed by me. To do so would mean division. There should be only one major in one school with deeper studies that go further and further, on and on.

Without boasting I can tell you that it is absolutely right to say that I follow Brother Nee. He laid the foundation for the recovery, and I surely follow him. However, in Brother Nee's time in the messages concerning God's desire, he went only as far as to use the term "God's plan." The term "God's economy" had not been touched at all yet. The concept of God's economy was brought in after we went to Taiwan. It is a further study and development of the same thing.

In addition, in Brother Nee's time the Lord showed us

that Christ is the Spirit, but it was not until after we went
to Taiwan that the Lord pointed out to us that the last
Adam became the life-giving Spirit. According to my
memory in all our messages before 1950 such a point was
never touched. Again, this point does not differ, but it goes
on.

Furthermore, I can testify that Brother Nee emphasized
the Spirit to the uttermost, but he never stressed the matter
of the seven Spirits particularly. The point concerning the
seven Spirits was not touched in a thorough way until 1969
in Erie, Pennsylvania. This point, however, was not
touched in a way that differs from Brother Nee's teaching,
but rather in a way that goes on to build something further
upon the same foundation.

It is true that I have been following Brother Nee all the
time but I have never invented any new major, and I have
never set up any other school. Before I contacted Brother
Nee and became a co-worker under him, I had a good
Christian work of my own in North China. If you knew the
situation there at that time, you would realize that there
was a big opening for my work in all of North China.
Apart from some in my hometown of Chefoo, there was not
one adequate Bible teacher there. Chefoo was well-known
as a center for Bible teaching in all of North China mainly
because of the Brethren assembly there, which I attended
for seven and a half years. Nevertheless, according to my
opinion, the kind of works they had might not have been
up to the standard of what God was enabling me to do.

Before I went to Shanghai to join the work with Brother
Nee, I was invited to dinner with the leading pastor in our
city. At that time he made a special request that I not set
up our group as a church, but that we keep our hall and
teach the Bible there six evenings a week, from Monday
through Saturday. Then on the Lord's Day he wanted me
to close that hall, and he assured me that I would be
invited and welcomed by all of the denominations in

Chefoo. He even told me that I would be exalted to the uttermost, and that many people would benefit from my teaching. Of course, I could not consider doing such a thing.

By the Lord's mercy I was given the ability to teach the Bible in a very adequate way. Even before I went to Shanghai to join Brother Nee in his work, I had expounded the Song of Songs. Of course, at that time I did not know much about Christ, the Spirit, life, and the church, but I might have become an expert in teaching typology, prophecy, and the dispensations of the Bible. If I would have simply taught these things, I could have become an expert in North China in teaching the Bible in this way. Also, there was a big opening for me to do this. Nevertheless, by the Lord's mercy, after I contacted Brother Nee, I began to see that God's way is not in typology, nor in prophecy, nor in biblical dispensations, but in Christ as the Spirit and as life for the church. When I came into such a vision, I absolutely dropped everything else and simply followed Brother Nee.

I dropped everything to the uttermost to follow Brother Nee. Whatever he spoke, I spoke. Whatever he taught, I taught. Whatever he preached, I preached. I am one hundred percent in tune with him. Some people have said in a somewhat accusing and mocking way that I imitate Watchman Nee. However, to me it is marvelous to hear others say this. They are absolutely right to say that I imitate him. In my gestures, my way of expression, the terms I used, even in the accent and how fast or slow I spoke, I simply imitated Watchman Nee in every way. I consider it glorious that I could imitate such a servant of the Lord who had the heavenly vision concerning the Lord's move on earth.

By the Lord's mercy, I was studying in Watchman Nee's field all the time. He was my professor, and I was his student. We were in the same major. How could you be a student under a professor who is teaching in one field with one major and be studying in another field with another major, trying to make yourself different from your professor and more significant than he is? How could this be?

I believe this illustration of a major field of study is very good. We are all in one school, in one field, with one major. The only difference between the professor and the students is that the professor is now teaching them. They may go on from him, but they should not go away from him. It is right and proper for them to go on to build up the same thing higher and higher, richer and richer.

How I thank the Lord for this way. If I had not followed Watchman Nee but had remained in my own ability to teach the Bible in my own way, I believe I could have gained a name for myself, but that would have been the end. All that would have come of that teaching would have been merely a name for myself. I would have missed the Lord's way and His rich blessing in His own way, and my teaching would not have been a part of God's New Testament ministry.

I would strongly encourage all of you to keep yourselves strictly in the same major and persevere there. You should not think differently, but go on further in the same major. No need to say in the twenty-seven books of the New Testament, even in the fourteen books of Paul you could dig out a number of points concerning the incarnation of Christ and concerning His human living.

Third, you need to study all the points concerning the death of Christ. This is a vast subject that needs much study. Then you need to study all the points concerning Christ's resurrection and the points concerning His ascension.

Then you need further study to cover all the points concerning the Person of Christ. In this study you will see that His Person eventually consummates in the life-giving Spirit. Furthermore, you need to develop this item, the life-giving

Spirit, in Paul's books. If you spend two years to study the other items, His incarnation, His human living, His death, His resurrection, His ascension, and His Person, you need to spend more years to study Christ being consummated in the life-giving Spirit. In addition, for this point you need to study the human spirit.

Another major point in the study of Paul's Epistles is the church. Under this subject you need to study the producing of the church, the nature of the church, including the life, the essence, of the church, and the building up of the church. You need to study the function of the church and also the different titles of the church. We need to realize, brothers, that to cover even the points we have already mentioned adequately may take nearly ten years.

Sorry to say, brothers, I am afraid that you have taken an easy way. Because we have spent so much time together, and because you have been under my training for years, it is easy for me to say a frank word of love to you. Sometimes you use my messages to constitute a message for you to give. That is wonderful, but because you take an easy way in doing it, you cannot make your message interesting. Your presentation of the Life-studies in this way does not stir up the people's interest. Therefore, you turn away from the Life-studies to other things in order to attract a crowd.

THE LORD'S BLESSING ON A
PARTICULAR KIND OF WORK

From the day I began the work in Taiwan, I had no intention to stir up the people's interest and no intention to gather a crowd. I am not narrow, and I am not demanding, but I do mean business in the Lord's work. My burden in beginning the work there was simply to carry out God's New Testament ministry. The Lord blessed the work there, and many of you here were captured by the Lord and became trainees under my teaching there. Although I had no intention to gather a crowd, eventually a very large number were gathered there in Taiwan.

According to recent reliable statistics showing the number in the different churches in Taiwan, the number of those meeting with us is second only to the number in the Scottish Presbyterian Church, which has been in Taiwan for more than a century. Their number is listed as over 87,000, but a good many among them are not saved. The number of those meeting with us is listed as 45,000, and the third largest is the True Jesus Church with 20,000.

My point is this. Although I had no intention to gather a crowd, eventually forty-five thousand were gathered. The number has not gone up much in the last twenty-two years since I left Taiwan. I was there just over ten years, and the number was very close to forty thousand when I left Taiwan to come to the United States.

After this experience, when I see you try to take up other fields, other majors, and leave the school of Christ and the church, I cannot tolerate it. All of us need to come back to the original school and stay in the original major, Christ and the church. We need some further study in this one major. You can use the Life-studies of the Bible as a help, as a base, for your study, but each one of you needs to study the Word of God in a thorough way for yourself for this major. What you need is a very thorough study of the divine revelation with the help of the Life-studies of the Bible. I would beg you all not to try to do an easy work in the Lord's recovery.

MAINTAINING THE FRESHNESS BY TURNING AWAY FROM ANY LIGHT WORK, ANY EASY WAY

In the Lord's recovery, or even in any field of scientific study today there is no easy work. If any of the professors in the universities tried to do an easy work, they could not get the results they need. Therefore, I encourage you all to go back to study all the aforementioned crucial points in Paul's fourteen Epistles with the help of the Life-studies. Then you will see what comes out.

I do believe, dear brothers, that if you get into such a study, not only fresh apprehension but also fresh feeling will enrich you. You will be refreshed with sweet feelings. Then you may go to the meeting to present the same thing I presented, but you would present it in a way that is more and more refreshing and sweetened.

On the other hand, if you take an easy way by going to the Life-studies merely to learn some points to present in the church meeting, that means nothing. In fact, that way could be compared to committing suicide, because you simply kill yourself. Then, if you would go to other fields, leaving the field of Christ and the church, that would mean that you drop the Lord's recovery. The Lord's recovery is not narrow, but it is very strict. To be narrow is one thing, but to be strict is another matter altogether. Those of you who have graduated from college know that you must be strict in your major; otherwise, you can never advance, you cannot make progress.

In Paul's writings we can see Christ's incarnation, Christ's human living, His death, His resurrection, His ascension, and, in addition, how He as such a One became the all-inclusive, life-giving Spirit. This matter is altogether related to our spirit in our experience. Therefore, we need to study the human spirit.

CHRIST AS LIFE AND THE EXPERIENCE OF CHRIST IN PAUL'S WRITINGS

Two further points are more than crucial in Paul's writings and in his part of the New Testament ministry. One is the matter of Christ being life to us, and the other is our experience of Christ. Although the Gospel of John is a Gospel of life, Christ being life to us cannot be seen there in a very practical way. In the Gospel of John we are told only that this Son of God is life, and that He came that we might have life and have it more abundantly (John 1:4; 14:6; 10:10). That is all. For this matter we need to come to the Epistles of Paul. In his fourteen Epistles, here and there and bit by bit, Paul gives a complete picture showing us how Christ is our experience in a practical way. You need to study this matter. In addition, no other books convey the details concerning how we experience Christ. The experience of Christ is presented in detail in Paul's writings. You need to spend much time to study this one aspect.

THE CHURCH'S CONSTITUTION WITH CHRIST AS THE SPIRIT TO BE OUR LIFE

In addition, in your study of the church and the very contents of the church, eventually you will realize that the content of the constitution of the church is actually of three aspects of one source. In the first place, the content of the church is of Christ. In addition, it is of the Spirit, and it is also of life. The church is constituted with Christ as the Spirit to be our life. The source of the content of the church and also the very constituents of the constitution of the church are Christ, the Spirit, and life. First you need to study how Christ is the source, the very constituent for the constitution of the church in the fourteen Epistles of Paul. Then, in the same way you need to study how the life-giving Spirit is the source and the constituent of the constitution of the church, and, further, how the divine life, the *zoe* life, is the source and the constituent of the constitution of the church.

All of these items are big and crucial aspects in Paul's writings, and all of them have not been covered adequately. I have simply given you some illustrations or some hints to help you study these fourteen Epistles. In these matters I do not encourage you to study all the twenty-seven books of the New Testament at this time. Simply by studying

Paul's writings, you will be very much enriched, and all the churches under your teaching will be enriched. How much we need this enriching so that none of us will be poor any longer. There is no need to pick up subjects other than the ones we have mentioned. The riches are here.

PAUL'S QUALIFICATION FOR HIS PART IN THE CONTINUATION OF THE MINISTRY FOR THE PRODUCING OF THE CHURCH

The crucial point we need to see is that Paul's part in the New Testament ministry is exactly the continuation of the section of the ministry of the Lord Jesus. The only difference is that the Lord used Paul to go on further from Christ to the church. In the Acts and Epistles we have seen clearly that the Lord used Peter to continue His own ministry, but we must say that Peter somewhat became stuck to the oldness. The Lord always knows the real situation. By that time the Lord knew that there was no way for Peter to go on. Therefore, the Lord needed a new one, someone who would drop anything old. That one was Saul of Tarsus. The Acts and the Epistles show us clearly how the Lord used Paul to go on further from Christ to the church.

This is the New Testament ministry. From the initiation of John the Baptist, the New Testament ministry goes on to Christ as its major part and its foundation. From that point there was the need for a new one to go further to produce the church, to build the church, and to have a Body to express Christ. This is a crucial point.

THE UP-TO-DATE CONTINUATION OF THE NEW TESTAMENT MINISTRY

Brother Nee gave a series of messages on the Body of Christ, and I would say that the matter of the Body was covered adequately to the fullest in those messages. Nevertheless, in Brother Nee's time some of the points that we have seen today were not touched. One point that was

not touched was the fullness of Him who fills all in all
(Eph. 1:23). The fullness of Christ was not touched, nor
was the matter of the fullness of God, which is the church
(Eph. 4:13; 3:19). It was not until we moved to Taiwan that
the Lord began to show us that the Body of Christ is the
fullness, not only of Him, but also of God. In Brother Nee's
time we did not have a clear and adequate definition of the
term fullness. In addition, even the matter of "the
unsearchable riches of Christ" was not emphasized in his
time. I do not believe you could find this expression in any
of Brother Nee's writings that have been published.

Surely Brother Nee did his best to present the Lord's
recovery to us, and I can certainly testify that he did his
uttermost. I am surely grateful to him, but in these past
thirty-five years there has been a continuation. No new
field has been opened, and no other major has been set up
for you to study. The major, Christ and the church, has
remained the same; nevertheless, again and again this
major has been further developed. This is a crucial point,
and all of us surely need to pay attention to this matter. I
believe these points help us to understand Paul's part of
the New Testament ministry.

Paul's part of the New Testament ministry is to
minister Christ as the incarnated One, as the One who
lived a particular, special, wonderful, excellent human life
on this earth. This One died a death that is all-inclusive,
and He entered into His resurrection in which He became
the life-giving Spirit who indwells our spirit to make us
members of Christ in order that a Body could be formed to
be the fullness of Him who fills all in all for the full
expression of Christ. This is Paul's part in the New
Testament ministry. If we are clear concerning this matter,
we will know where the Lord's recovery stands today.

CHAPTER SEVEN

PETER'S AND JOHN'S PARTS IN THE NEW TESTAMENT MINISTRY

We have traced the New Testament ministry from its initiation with John the Baptist through its foundation and its major part with the Lord Jesus Himself and on to its continuation and further development with the Apostle Paul. In this chapter we come to Peter's part in the New Testament ministry from his two Epistles and to John's part from his Epistles and from the book of Revelation, which is the consummation of the entire Bible.

OUR PRAYER

Lord, we thank You for this gathering; we have the assurance that You are with us. Grant us the mercy and the grace, Lord, that we may practice being one spirit with You. We pray that You would be one with us and that we may be one with You, even right now in this meeting, in the sharing, in the testimonies, in the speaking.

Lord, we pray that Your word might be so clear to us, that we may see what is in Your heart, what is revealed in Your Word. Lord, grant us a sober mind, a seeking heart, and an open spirit. O Lord, we need You; we need Your word, and we need Your unveiling. Lord, do unload us, and take away all the veils, all the distractions. We trust in You, Lord, and we trust in Your blessing. Lord, everything is altogether up to You; we are here waiting on You. We pray that You would do something and work upon all of us. Amen.

PETER AND THE DIVINE LIFE

In such a spirit and with such a prayer before the Lord, we want to continue our fellowship concerning the New Testament ministry. We all need to be clear that the line of Peter's two books is life, the divine life, the spiritual life, the life that is the very Triune God being imparted into us. Without such a word I am afraid it would be hard for any one of you to tell what the line of Peter's two Epistles is, even after we have completed our Life-study on them in our training.

The first point that indicates that this divine life is the line of Peter's two books is the fact that Peter strongly emphasized that we have been regenerated with the incorruptible seed (1 Pet. 1:3, 23). Surely this regeneration is a matter of life. Then in chapter two of his first Epistle Peter tells us that Christ carried up our sins in His body onto the cross in order that we might live (v. 24). Here Peter does not say that Christ died on the cross that we might be forgiven, but he says that we might live. Peter's word here corresponds to the Lord's word in John 3:14-15 that says that the Son of Man will be lifted up as Moses lifted up the brass serpent in the wilderness, that we may have eternal life.

THE GRACE OF LIFE AND A LIVING OF SHEPHERDING

Furthermore, Peter even says that the grace we received is the grace of life (1 Pet. 3:7). Even the weaker vessels, referring to the sisters in this verse, are the heirs of the grace of life. The grace of life is God as life and life supply to us in His Trinity—the Father as the source of life, the Son as the course of life, and the Spirit as the flow of life flowing within us with the Son and the Father. All believers are heirs of this grace. In brief, the grace of life is the Triune God processed to become the all-inclusive, life-giving, indwelling Spirit. The Triune God is now within us as the grace of life (See footnote 7[5] in 1 Pet. 3—Recovery Version and pp. 210-211 of Message 23, Life-study of First Peter.) Paul also touched the matter of the grace of life, but never expressed it in these terms. You cannot find the expression "the grace of life" in Paul's writings, but you can see the same thing covered in Romans 5. Paul used these two words, grace and life, in Romans 5:21, but he never composed these two words together into a phrase, the grace of life.

Chapter four of 1 Peter also has some hint concerning life (see vv. 1-2, 6). Then in chapter five Peter's exhortation concerning the eldership is altogether related to the living of the elders. Surely what Peter presents in these verses is altogether not merely in the realm of teaching or of practice (vv. 1-3). Peter exhorts the elders to live a life, which is their shepherding. The proper shepherding should be the elders' living. The elders live a life that is an example for the flock and that example is the shepherding of the flock. The example or pattern for the flock is a life (5:3). You can never shepherd a church in a way that is apart from the way you live. If you do not live in a certain way, you can never shepherd the church in that way. This is life. The Epistles of Peter are on the line of life.

THE DEVELOPMENT OF ALL THE ITEMS OF LIFE

The first few verses of the first chapter of 2 Peter tell us that God has given us all the things relating to life. How much I appreciate these verses! At the time of our regeneration God has given us all the various aspects of the divine life. We may say that regeneration brings in the richest deposit, for through regeneration God has deposited into us a full supply of His riches of life to be what we may call our "capital." Because God has already given us all the things concerning life, what we need now is to develop what we have received, not to receive these things again. According to 2 Peter 1:3-8, in the initial item of life given to us, we need to develop the second item. Then in the second, we need to develop the third, and in the third, the fourth. We need to go on to further develop all the items of life, one after another, until we reach the eighth item. With such a development in life we will have a rich entry into the kingdom.

A CONTINUATION OF THE LINE OF LIFE

Even 2 Peter 1 is adequate to show us that Peter is in the line of life and that his ministry is a continuation of the ministry of the Lord Jesus. Peter had seen the Lord's ministry when He was on this earth, and Peter continued in the same line.

In Peter's fifth message recorded in Acts, he also spoke of life. When he related the story to the Jewish believers of how he saw the Spirit fall on those in the house of Cornelius while he was speaking, he concluded by saying that he realized that the Gentiles could also repent to have life (Acts 11:18). We should not consider that Peter's ministry is something away from the line of life. Peter did not go away from the line of life. We always consider that it is John's ministry, his Gospel and his Epistles, that is on the line of life. Surely John is on the line of life, but Peter is also on the same line.

PETER'S RECOMMENDING OF PAUL'S MINISTRY

Furthermore, I would say a strong word concerning the way Peter confirmed and recommended Paul's ministry in the last chapter of his second book (2 Pet. 3:15-16). He told us clearly that in Paul's writings there are some deep points that are hard for people to understand. The way Peter refers to "our beloved brother Paul" and highly commends Paul's writings indicates that Peter was for Paul's ministry. (See last paragraph of footnote 16^2 in 2 Pet. 3—Recovery Version.) Paul's ministry is on Christ and the church, which is constituted of Christ, of the Spirit, and of life, that the church might be the expression of the Triune God. Therefore, by this confirmation and recommendation of Paul's ministry you can see how much Peter's part of the New Testament ministry is one with the Lord's part and with Paul's part.

THE DIVINE LIFE AND ITS FELLOWSHIP
IN JOHN'S FIRST EPISTLE

John's part of the New Testament ministry is also on the line of life. John's first Epistle is simply marvelous. We all need to see that this is a book on life and on the divine fellowship of this divine life. First John unveils to us that in our experience and for our experience there are three points of the divine life: the fellowship, the anointing, and the birth. Because the training on John's Epistles adequately covered these points, we do not need to say much here, but I would encourage you all to spend some time to study 1 John with the help of the notes of the Recovery Version and the Life-study messages. You need to saturate yourselves with these three matters of the divine life: the fellowship of the divine life, the anointing of the divine life, and the birth of the divine life.

Through the birth of this divine life, we have received a divine seed. The word seed is used by John in a particular way. In this divine seed are virtues, including the virtue to practice God's righteousness, the virtue to practice God's love, and the virtue to overcome sin, the world, and Satan. We need to remember that 1 John is on (1) the divine life, (2) its fellowship, (3) its anointing, and (4) its birth with the seed to provide us the virtues in three things—righteousness, love, and victory. If you get into these few points, the entire book will become your constituents so that you are constituted with this divine life.

THE CONSUMMATION IN REVELATION

In John's last book, we come to a threefold consummation—the consummation of John's writings, the consummation of the New Testament, and even the consummation of the entire Bible. As such a consummation, the book of Revelation is crucial. As a part of God's New Testament ministry, this book has never been opened up so much as it has been since 1969, which was the time the Lord showed us the seven Spirits.

The first important principle in understanding the book of Revelation is that nearly every item in this book has been presented already either in the Old Testament or in the other books of the New Testament. You may be surprised or even shocked to realize that, basically, Revelation does not present anything new.

The Lampstands

For example, the first point in the book of Revelation is the lampstands (Rev. 1:12, 20; 2:1). In the Old Testament there were lampstands in the tabernacle in Exodus and in the temple in 1 Kings (Exo. 25:31-40; 1 Kings 7:49). Furthermore, in Zechariah there is the lampstand with the seven lamps as the seven eyes of the stone of grace (3:9; 4:2, 10). Therefore, this term, the lampstand, is not a new expression in Revelation but is clearly from the Old Testament. (See also Matt. 5:15.) Whatever is found in Revelation is not a new item, but rather the full development of a particular item that has been presented already. The lampstand is not developed to its fullest extent until the book of Revelation.

The Throne and the New Jerusalem

Another illustration of this principle is the throne of God with the four living creatures before the throne (Rev. 4:2, 6-11; 5:6). These are not new items, because Ezekiel had seen and described them long before (Ezek. 1:5-26). Item after item which is presented in Revelation is the full development of something already presented in the Old Testament. This principle is crucial for our understanding of this book.

Even the New Jerusalem is not a new item in the book of Revelation. At the end of Ezekiel there is a city with twelve gates, a city called "The Lord is there" (Ezek. 48:30-35). The city with twelve gates is an old item renewed and developed in Revelation (Rev. 21:12-13). You may be surprised and even shocked to find that one item after another in Revelation is not new but is rather a further development of something already presented. Without this principle, you cannot understand this mysterious book.

The Development of the Revelation Concerning the Divine Trinity

Furthermore, even the revelation concerning the divine Trinity has been developed in the book of Revelation. In Matthew we see the Father, the Son, and the Spirit (28:19). In theology, to indicate the Father you simply say the First in the Trinity, and everyone understands that you are speaking of the Father. Likewise, the Second is Christ the Son, and the Third is the Spirit. However, when we come to the first chapter of Revelation the sequence of the divine Trinity is altogether changed. Verse 4 says, "from Him Who is, and Who was, and Who is coming." This expression, "Him Who is, and Who was, and Who is coming," is triune and is equivalent to the Old Testament expression for Jehovah (Exo. 3:14). In the divine Trinity revealed in this book, the first One is triune and is Jehovah, the great Eternal, the great I Am, the great To Be, the One who is, who was, and who is coming, or who is to be. Therefore, even from this one point we can see that the divine Trinity is very much developed.

After naming first Him who is, and who was, and who is coming, verse 4 continues, "And from the seven Spirits Who are before His throne." Here the Second is not the Son, but the Spirit, and the Spirit here is not one Spirit but seven Spirits, a sevenfold development. In the development of the divine Trinity in Revelation 1:4, the First becomes Jehovah, and the Second becomes the seven Spirits. The Third is in verse 5, "And from Jesus Christ, the faithful Witness, the Firstborn of the dead, and the Ruler of the kings of the earth." Here the Third is not the Spirit, but the Son. This indicates that the sequence of the divine Trinity is altogether changed. The faithful Witness refers to the Son's earthly life, and the Firstborn of the dead refers to His resurrection. In addition, the Ruler of the kings of the earth refers to His ascension, to His present situation, and to His coming back.

Moreover, neither the term "the Father" nor the term "the Son" is used in these two verses, and the Spirit is mentioned as "the seven Spirits." Surely this is the fullest development of the divine Trinity, showing that all the creeds are inadequate. If you are going to accept any of the creeds, it is as if you need to cut your long feet to make them fit into a pair of short shoes.

In Revelation the divine Trinity is not a new thing. At least in Matthew 28:19 the matter of the divine Trinity has been developed. In fact, from Genesis 1:1 the divine Trinity has been developed through all the books up to Matthew 28:19 and has been applied in the Acts, in the Epistles, and all the way to the book of Revelation. Now at the very opening word of this book you have the fullest development of the divine Trinity. Moreover, the development continues in chapters four and five, where we are told that the seven Spirits are the seven lamps before the throne of God (4:5) as well as the seven eyes of the Lamb (5:6). The seven lamps before the throne are for God's administration over the entire universe; the seven eyes of the Lamb are for Christ's observing, judging, and infusing. What a further development of the divine Trinity this is! In the development of the divine Trinity, the Spirit becomes the eyes of the Son. The One called the Third in traditional theology becomes the eyes of the Second. How could you explain such a thing? Are they two Persons or one? Surely the light in these few verses annuls the entire teaching of the traditional theology concerning the three Persons. According to the terminology of traditional theology, if the third Person becomes the eyes of the second Person, you would lose one Person, so that eventually you would have only two Persons among the divine Trinity. How could you count your eyes as a separate person from yourself? This one matter gives you a strong reason not to follow the traditional teaching concerning the divine Trinity.

I have especially encouraged the young people to study Greek for the purpose of going on to see further things in the pure Word of God, not to go back to study those traditional things. The verses we have been considering illustrate the way to get into the pure Word of God apart from any influence of traditional teaching. Even our brief consideration of these few verses in Revelation leaves no ground for the erroneous teaching that the Father, the Son, and the Spirit are three separate Persons. In fact, it destroys that wrong teaching.

The Fullest Unveiling of the Church

Furthermore, the book of Revelation uses the developed Trinity for the fullest unveiling of the church. Revelation 1:4 begins, "John to the seven churches." You need to take note of the word seven. "To the seven churches ... from Him Who is, and Who was, and Who is coming, and from the seven Spirits." Again, you need to take note of the word seven. The seven Spirits match the seven churches, the seven churches are the seven lampstands (1:20), and the seven Spirits are the seven eyes of the Lamb (5:6). The church in its fullest development is the seven churches as the seven lampstands which need the seven Spirits as the seven eyes of the Lamb to match them.

Christ Developed with Seven Eyes

In Revelation even Christ has been developed. He did not have seven eyes when He was on this earth. Peter and James did not see the seven eyes. John who reclined on the bosom of Christ surely saw the Lord Jesus with only two eyes, but in Revelation, he saw the seven eyes of the Lamb. The seven eyes are a development. The One who used to have two eyes now has seven eyes.

The church in its fullest development needs to be matched by Christ in His development, and this matching is altogether a matter of the seven Spirits. This point is crucial. For the matching to be a matter of the seven

Spirits means that we need not only to be filled but also to be saturated and even soaked in the seven Spirits. Then the church becomes the lampstand.

The Lampstand as the Embodiment of the Triune God

The lampstand is the embodiment of the Triune God. From 1975 we began to see the lampstand as the embodiment of the Triune God with three aspects—the substance, the form, and the expression. The substance of the lampstand is gold. In fact, the entire lampstand is a lump of gold (Rev. 1:12; Exo. 25:31). Gold signifies the divine substance, which is God Himself. This lump of gold also has a form. It is not merely a bare piece of gold but a piece of gold in a definite form with a purpose. The gold is in the form of a lampstand, and this form signifies Christ. God took a definite form in His Son. Actually, the Son of God is the form of God. In addition, the seven lamps are the expression of the lampstand. Both Zechariah and Revelation tell us that the seven lamps are the seven Spirits (Zech. 4:2, 10; Rev. 4:5). Therefore, these seven lamps that are the expression of the lampstand signify the seven Spirits, that is, the Spirit of God. Based upon the Spirit as the expression of the lampstand, it is clear that the lampstand is the embodiment of the Triune God, the embodiment of the Father as the substance, of the Son as the form, and of the Spirit as the expression.

In Revelation the lampstands specifically signify not Christ but the church. (See footnote 12[3] in Rev. 1—Recovery Version.) Nevertheless, we should not say that the lampstands are not Christ; rather, we should say that the lampstands are the increase of Christ. In Exodus 25 only Christ was typified in the lampstand, but in Revelation Christ in His increase is signified in the lampstands. The lampstands in Revelation signify Christ in His enlargement, in His increase.

When we are talking about the ministry of the New Testament, we need to ask ourselves whether we know how to minister the embodiment of the Triune God as the very solid element of the church. We need to consider this matter soberly. Including myself, I would say that we do not know much about this matter.

We need to see what the ground is for saying that Christ with His seven eyes is for the churches in the fullest development. At least once in writing to a church in the two chapters following chapter one, Christ declares that He has the seven Spirits (3:1). The fact that He has the seven Spirits indicates that what He has is to match the seven churches, and now the seven churches are the seven lampstands in the fullest development of the church.

The Development of the Churches

In this book there is a long parenthetical section from chapter four through chapter twenty. The first three chapters of Revelation are the basic chapters on the church, and the last two chapters are the basic chapters on the consummation of the church. In between is a long parenthesis of seventeen chapters that tells of God's dealing with the universe by His governmental administration. This parenthetical section begins with the throne of God (4:2) and ends with Satan cast into the lake of fire (20:10). What is indicated in this section is God's dealing with His enemy, from the throne to the lake of fire.

During the time that God is dealing with His enemy, the churches are going on in growth. Therefore, even in the parenthetical section of seventeen chapters there are several references to the church people. In chapter seven is the innumerable multitude of believers, and in chapter twelve are the woman with the manchild (7:9; 12:1, 5). In chapter fourteen are the firstfruit with the harvest, in chapter fifteen are the overcomers on the glassy sea, and in chapter nineteen is the wife of the Lamb (14:4, 15; 15:2; 19:7-8). Then in chapter twenty are the overcoming saints who will be co-kings with Christ in the millennium (v. 6). These references to the church people within God's governmental dealings indicate that the church is being developed during the time that God's governmental dealing with His enemy is going on. These six instances—the innumerable multitude, the woman with the man-child, the firstfruit with the harvest, the overcoming ones on the glassy sea, the wife of the Lamb, and the co-kings of Christ in the millennium—show that the church is still going on and being developed while God is dealing with Satan.

The New Jerusalem

Eventually, when God has finished dealing with His enemy, the church will come into its fullest consummation in the new heaven and the new earth—the New Jerusalem. Therefore, we need to go on from the lampstand to the New Jerusalem. In the lampstand you can see the embodiment of the Triune God but not all the riches detailed in the Triune God applied to His church. In the New Jerusalem, you can see all the riches of the Triune God applied to His redeemed.

There the Triune God is flowing as the water of life, and the very embodiment of the Triune God, Christ as the Lamb, is the tree of life growing along the flowing river of life (22:1-2). There in the New Jerusalem you can also see God in the Lamb as the light to His redeemed (21:23). These three things, the river of life, the tree of life, and the light of life, will be the intrinsic essences of the living of the New Jerusalem. We need to see that the New Jerusalem will live by these three essences. The river of life, the tree of life, and the light of life are all of the essence of life. (For more details concerning the New Jerusalem, see chapters eight through eleven of *The Basic Revelation in the Holy Scriptures*.)

In conclusion, we need to consider what the part of John's ministry is in the New Testament ministry. When we consider this matter, we have to confess that there is nothing that we can say because we are short. Compared with this part of the New Testament ministry, we ourselves are in kindergarten. What poverty there is today compared with this part of the New Testament ministry! We have to confess that we are poor.

THE RECOVERY OF THE UNIQUE MINISTRY OF THE NEW TESTAMENT

If you are burdened to go on in the New Testament ministry of God, you need to go on along this line, in this major, and in this school. I strongly encourage you not to get out of this school, not to get off from this major, and not to get on any other line. Here is a strong major in the unique school for you to explore in your spiritual study. In this line is what the Lord needs, and in this line you will never cause trouble. Your going on in this line will edify the saints, build up the church, and build up the Body to its fullest extent. Furthermore, it will never create any division or any confusion. If you take another way, you will be out of the unique school, off from this major, and not in the line of the New Testament ministry. In that case, whatever you preach, whatever you teach, and whatever you present will be a cause of division. I encourage you to consider this matter soberly.

In the Lord's recovery, if we were to control people merely so that we could present our teaching, that would be foolish, and it would be low or mean. No one can control people except a strong sect. Nearly all of the denominations exercise control over their preachers. For example, if you are going to be a preacher in a certain denomination, it is necessary for you to preach their teaching. Now we need to consider what is the teaching in the Lord's recovery, whether it is Witness Lee's teaching, Watchman Nee's teaching, or some other teaching. It is on this point that I am burdened. We need to be very clear that we do not have anyone's teaching. We are in the Lord's recovery, and His recovery is to recover His unique ministry. This unique ministry is the ministry of the New Testament, which is to minister the Triune God embodied in Christ as life into His chosen people to make them living members to form the Body of Christ to express Christ as the very embodiment of the Triune God. If we say that we have some kind of teaching, surely this New Testament ministry is our unique teaching, and this ministry should control our preaching and our teaching. We are not controlled by any sectarian denominational teaching, but we should be controlled by this unique New Testament ministry.

What we have seen in these seven chapters is the ministry of the New Testament of God. With this ministry as our basis, we will go on to see what the vision in the Lord's recovery is today. Then we will have a ground, a view, and even a standard of measurement so that we will know where to stay, where to go, and where to be limited.